# SIGNS
# AND SECRETS
## OF THE
# MESSIAH

## A FRESH LOOK AT THE MIRACLES OF JESUS

# RABBI JASON SOBEL

W PUBLISHING GROUP

AN IMPRINT OF THOMAS NELSON

Published in Nashville, Tennessee, by W Publishing Group, an imprint of Thomas Nelson.

Thomas Nelson titles may be purchased in bulk for educational, business, fundraising, or sales promotional use. For information, please email SpecialMarkets@ThomasNelson.com.

Unless otherwise noted, Scripture quotations are taken from the Holy Scriptures, Tree of Life Version. Copyright © 2014, 2016 by the Tree of Life Bible Society. Used by permission of the Tree of Life Bible Society.

Scripture quotations marked CJB are taken from the Complete Jewish Bible by David H. Stern. © 1998. All rights reserved. Used by permission of Messianic Jewish Publishers, 6120 Day Long Lane, Clarksville, MD 21029.

Scripture quotations marked ESV are from the ESV® Bible (The Holy Bible, English Standard Version®). Copyright © 2001 by Crossway, a publishing ministry of Good News Publishers. Used by permission. All rights reserved.

Scripture quotations marked MSG are taken from THE MESSAGE. Copyright © 1993, 2002, 2018 by Eugene H. Peterson. Used by permission of NavPress. All rights reserved. Represented by Tyndale House Publishers, a Division of Tyndale House Ministries.

Scripture quotations marked NASB are taken from the New American Standard Bible® (NASB). Copyright © 1960, 1962, 1963, 1968, 1971, 1972, 1973, 1975, 1977, 1995, 2020 by The Lockman Foundation. Used by permission. All rights reserved.

Scripture quotations marked NIV are taken from the Holy Bible, New International Version®, NIV®. © 1973, 1978, 1984, 2011 by Biblica, Inc.® Used by permission of Zondervan. All rights reserved worldwide. www. zondervan.com. The "NIV" and "New International Version" are trademarks registered in the United States Patent and Trademark Office by Biblica, Inc.®

Scripture quotations marked NKJV are taken from the New King James Version®. © 1982 by Thomas Nelson. Used by permission. All rights reserved.

Scripture quotations marked NLT are taken from the Holy Bible, New Living Translation, © 1996, 2004, 2015 by Tyndale House Foundation. Used by permission of Tyndale House Publishers, a Division of Tyndale House Ministries, Carol Stream, Illinois 60188. All rights reserved.

Scripture quotations marked THE VOICE are taken from The Voice™. Copyright © 2012 by Ecclesia Bible Society. Used by permission. All rights reserved.

Boldface added to Scripture quotations are the author's emphasis.

Any internet addresses, phone numbers, or company or product information printed in this book are offered as a resource and are not intended in any way to be or to imply an endorsement by Thomas Nelson, nor does Thomas Nelson vouch for the existence, content, or services of these sites, phone numbers, companies, or products beyond the life of this book.

ISBN 978-0-7852-4025-9 (audiobook)
ISBN 978-0-7852-4024-2 (eBook)
ISBN 978-0-7852-4023-5 (HC)
ISBN 978-0-7852-4021-1 (TP)

**Library of Congress Control Number: 2023933799**

*Printed in the United States*

24 25 26 27 28 LBC 5 4 3 2 1

*To my wife, Miriam—your passion for the supernatural and pursuit of His Presence has been a continual source of inspiration. Thank you for being such a wonderful wife and woman of faith.*

*To Ted Squires—you're the best! I'm profoundly grateful for your sacrificial support and your steady encouragement. You're one in a trillion! Words can't express how much you and Terry mean to me. You are a visionary who always inspires me to dream bigger for God!*

# CONTENTS

# INTRODUCTION

I don't know about you, but I'm always excited to be involved in miracles. Miracles show us that Jesus (His Hebrew name is *Yeshua*) is alive and working powerfully in this skeptical world. I've witnessed authentic miracles in my own life and in others' lives. Nothing will ignite one's life like a miracle.

Some years ago, I received a phone call from a homeless friend in New York City. Jeff told me he had been sleeping on the cold streets of Chinatown during a New York winter night. As a result, he developed a horrific case of frostbite in both legs. He had been admitted to the hospital at New York University with the threat of never walking again and possible amputation. He was petrified, so my friend John and I rushed to the hospital to be with him.

I had recently read the *Besorah*—the accounts of the good news (the Gospels) found in the New Testament. I had read the book of Acts, and deep inside my heart, I knew that the Lord created me for the "greater [works] than these" (John 14:12) that Jesus promised. Greater works are our inheritance. To do greater works is our birthright. The followers of Yeshua prayed for people, and their prayers made people whole two thousand years ago. Why not here? Why not now? Why not us? If not you, who will walk in the authority Jesus entrusted to us?

We walked into Jeff's hospital room, where he was lying in bed, downcast and troubled. A blanket of icy depression chilled the atmosphere. His legs and feet were swollen and blistery and were a gruesome blackish green in color. Not only that but he was in severe pain.

As I gazed down at him lying there, a wave of compassion washed over me that was coming from a Source bigger than me, yet from inside me. I knew Jesus had promised in Matthew 25:40 that what we do for the "least of these," we are doing for God Himself. In that moment, it felt as if Jesus was watching me, nudging me on. I smiled and looked into Jeff's eyes. "Jeff," I said, "I really believe that God can heal you! Do you mind if we pray for you?"

Of course, he agreed.

I laid hands on him, essentially saying what Peter said in Acts 3:6: "Silver and gold have I none. But what I have in the name of Yeshua, rise, take up your bed, and walk!"

Nothing appeared to change at that moment, so we visited for a while and then left. A few days later, I received a phone call from Jeff. He excitedly told me that the hospital was sending him home and that he would be walking out of the hospital. There was nothing wrong with his legs! I'm sure the doctors were astounded. It typically takes six months or longer to recover from severe frostbite, if you recover at all. It was an absolute miracle—there's no other way to describe it.

If we are Christians, walking in the supernatural should be natural for us. Since it is within God's power, it should be part of His people's healthy, day-to-day spiritual life. Here's the question: How many of you need a miracle in your own life, or in the life of someone you care about? Well, you can have them! God has been doing miracles from the beginning of time. He did them throughout the Old Testament and the New Testament, and He will continue. He has never stopped. It's part of His character.

# Greater Miracles

The Old Testament prophet Micah told us, "As in the days of your coming out from the land of Egypt I will show him wonders" (7:15). What's significant in this verse is the idea that the miracles performed by the Messiah at the messianic redemption would be much greater and more numerous than the miracles performed by Moses. There were miracles in the past; there would be miracles in the future.

The purpose of this book is to help us see God's miracles from the book of John in a fresh new way that increases our faith in them for our own lives. You'll note that there are seven miracles in John's gospel, but I've chosen nine miracles or mysteries to cover because I didn't want to narrow Jesus' journey to only seven miracles. Some stories I share from John are miraculous mysteries and secrets that give us many thought-provoking applications.

# Signs, Miracles, and Secrets

The Bible says it's the "glory of God to conceal a matter and the glory of kings to search it out" (Prov. 25:2). As children of the King, we are called to immerse ourselves in the wonder and mystery of God's Word. The Bible is like a multifaceted diamond—its many sides contribute to its brilliance. There are many ways to read Bible text that are complementary and never contradictory. It's not worthless but worthwhile to look at every word from many angles.

The Bible is also like the ocean—shallow enough for any child and deep enough that you can't explore all of it. There are infinite layers to God's Word. That's what makes the Bible different from any other book written by a human author. There's always some new mystery or secret to be uncovered. That's why the Bible needs to be read repeatedly. It's not boring and should create a sense of wonder that renews your mind and transforms you.

Deeper spiritual truths are often not obvious on the surface, but they can be found, and it's the glory of the King to seek them out and meditate on them. Jesus gave us an example in the road-to-Emmaus experience (Luke 24). The more we look at languages, make connections between Old and New Testaments, and consider the numeric connections, the more secrets and mysteries (deeper meaning in the Scriptures) are revealed.

When discussing hidden secrets or mysteries, we're not attempting to make new doctrines based on these. We're merely wanting to go deeper in our study to determine what God is saying and what it means to us.

Throughout these pages, we will explore the depths of Yeshua's miracles and secrets. We will study them and discover how they changed lives back then and how His miracles and secrets are changing lives today.

Before you begin untangling this book, there are a few things you need to know that will help you on your journey.[1]

## Hebrew and Greek by the Numbers: The Code of Creation

Most of the world's languages separate numbers from letters, but not Hebrew and Greek. Both languages use letters—their respective alphabets—for numbers. Each letter in the Hebrew and Greek alphabets has a numeric value.[2] Because of this, numbers can spell words, and words add up to numeric values. So both words and numbers are significant as we study the mysteries and secrets in the Bible. Let me share some common questions people have about biblical letters and numbers.

**Why is it important to study the numbers?** The Bible often uses numbers in patterns, and there is significance to many of these patterns. For example, the first word of Genesis 1:1 is *bereisheet*, "in the beginning." The first letter of *bereisheet* is *bet*, which has a numeric value of 2. Why is it significant that the first letter in the Bible has a numeric value of 2? Because God created the world in twos. He created heaven and earth. He created light and dark. He created day and night. He created the sun and the moon. He created the sea and the dry ground. He created man and woman. The letter *bet* also represents blessing. Only when two opposites come together is God's blessing fully released.

**How can I study the Bible using numbers?** Here's an example of studying the significance of numbers in the Bible. The Lord told Moses to consecrate the Tabernacle for eight days. On each of the previous seven days, Moses erected the Tabernacle and took it down. But on the eighth day, the glory of God filled the Tabernacle after Moses and Aaron blessed the people (Lev. 9).

Why did the Lord choose the eighth day?

- 8 = the number of vestments worn by the high priest (Ex. 28)
- 8 = sprinklings of blood on *Yom Kippur* for atonement (Lev. 16:14–15)
- 8 = spices used in the Tabernacle, including the anointing oil and incense (Ex. 30:23–24, 34)
- 8 = instruments used by Levites, seven plus the voice of the choir[3]
- 8 = poles for carrying the holy vessels: the ark, the table, the golden altar, and the copper or brass altar (Ex. 25, 27, 39)

This repeated use of the number 8 created a consistency and pointed to the person and work of the Messiah. For example, Yeshua died and rose from the dead on a Sunday, which is both the first day and the eighth day. The Messiah died on Friday, which is the sixth day. Like the Father, He rested on the seventh day after finishing the work of redemption. Then He rose on the eighth day. Can you see how studying words and numbers can help you connect the Testaments and go deeper in your Bible study?

Connections such as these make the study of the Bible's original words and their associated numbers fascinating and life-changing.

## The Rabbis and Jewish Tradition

The Bible was written in a Jewish context. Jesus Himself was a Jew and a popular teacher of the Torah who was called "Rabbi" by the disciples and the crowds (Matt. 26:49; Mark 9:5; 10:51; 11:21; John 1:49; 20:16). Yet many Christians are unfamiliar with the Jewish interpretative tradition that forms part of the background for the New Testament. A better appreciation of this can lead to a richer understanding of both the Old and New Testaments.

The primary text of Judaism is the Old Testament (*Tanakh*), or the Hebrew Bible. The *Tanakh* has the same number of books as the Christian Bible's Old Testament, only they are arranged a bit differently. Much of the Hebrew Bible was handed down orally from generation to generation.

Jewish thought and Bible commentary are not a single or continuous tradition but rather a mixture of works from centuries of study. For several of the sources, the dating is even a mix of times. The writers reflected specific theological thoughts and historical positions. Also, many of the works were oral teachings that were later written.

What makes these works important is they represent Jewish thinking about the Bible and help us see things from different perspectives. These diverse perspectives are critical as you learn to connect the Old Testament with the New Testament. As Lois Tverberg pointed out, the insights of sages and rabbis from long ago help us understand that "Jesus was taking part in a tradition known for generations before his time. This makes all the difference in the world in terms of painting the Jewish reality around him."[4]

In this book I reference several sources from many centuries of Jewish thought. These sources help us examine and understand the Jewish meaning of many passages and their connection to the Messiah and New Testament. Just as Christian pastors and teachers use multiple sources to explain Scripture, we are bringing together essential sources to study the Messiah.

Around AD 200, Jewish scholars compiled the *Mishnah*—written text describing and explaining the Jewish law code that was mostly oral before that time.

Later, the Talmud, a collection of teachings and commentaries on Jewish law, was created. The Talmud contains the *Mishnah* and other texts, plus biblical interpretations from thousands of rabbis. They finalized the first Talmud around the third century AD. The rabbis completed a second edition in the fifth century AD.

*Midrash* is a Jewish method of interpreting Scripture as well as a compilation of such interpretations, which were composed between AD 400 and 1200. The Hebrew term *Midrash* comes from the biblical verb *darash*, which means "to seek out" or "to inquire." The rabbis were sensitive to the details in Scripture and therefore found meaning in every nuance of the text. For example, *Midrash* finds profound meaning and unique insights in words, letters, unusual spellings, phrases, missing letters, and so on. The rabbis, like good detectives, often questioned the text in pursuit of greater wisdom and truth. Midrashic insights never replace the literal meaning of the text but are intended to stand alongside it as an additional layer that clarifies a question, solves an issue in the text, or makes a practical application to the reader's life.

Judaism embraces many other texts and commentaries written by rabbis over the centuries. This book uses these to help connect the Old Testament to the New Testament. Since many manuscripts were compilations, we don't know who the scholars were. For that reason, this book includes references to "the rabbis" or "Jewish tradition" without specific citations or notes. Also, if there is a citation, it may be unfamiliar to the reader. For example, Babylonian Talmud 51 may be an accurate citation, but with so many translations, it's difficult to pinpoint the exact volume. Extensive research has gone into this book, and these rabbinical resources are invaluable for us to understand the connection and the secrets and mysteries of our Messiah Yeshua.

## The Tree of Life Version of the Bible

Most of the Scripture references in this book are from the Tree of Life Version of the Bible. The Tree of Life Version speaks with a decidedly Jewish-friendly voice—a voice like the Bible authors themselves—to recover the authentic context of the Scriptures and biblical faith. It was produced by messianic Jewish and Christian scholars who sought to highlight the rich Hebrew roots of the Christian faith. Since this translation restores the Jewish order and numbering of the books of the Old Testament, you may find that certain verse citations are one number off.

As we take this journey together, I pray God will lead you to new insights and breakthroughs and that He will reveal Himself to you with a sense of His presence and shalom.

# ONE

# THE SIGNS AND SECRETS
# OF TRANSFORMATION

All weddings are special occasions, but Jewish weddings are something to behold. There are some thirteen rituals during the traditional ceremony, ending with the celebratory dance called the *hora* as guests dance in a circle. At the same time, the bride and groom are seated on chairs and lifted into the air, waving handkerchiefs at the guests. As you can imagine, the blend of wine, food, Hebrew songs, and joy illuminates the atmosphere. I love officiating Jewish weddings because of all the festivities and emotions, but mainly because there's nothing like watching two single individuals become one in that holy moment. Barney Kasdan, rabbi at Kehilat Ariel Messianic Synagogue in San Diego, California, put it this way:

> Of all the customs appointed by God, there is probably none more joyous than that of the Jewish wedding. It is one simcha (joyous

occasion) that you do not want to miss! Of course, it is joyful enough to just witness the covenant vows between a man and woman who love each other. When you add family and friends, food, music and dance, it is difficult to find a more exuberant celebration.[1]

Messiah's first miracle occurred during a wedding, and it points to the abundance and blessing that come from our relationship with the Messiah Yeshua. His changing the water into wine was not merely a random act of kindness, as it may seem at first glance. God is sovereign over every seemingly insignificant detail, and the fact that this miracle involved wine and occurred at a Jewish wedding is highly significant.

## A Miracle in the Month of Miracles

The Jewish calendar is primarily broken into twelve months, just like the standard or Gregorian calendar we all use. The month of *Nisan* is the first month on the Jewish calendar according to the Torah, the five books of Moses (Ex. 12:2). *Nisan* coincides with the months March and April on a standard calendar. The Torah calls this month *chodesh ha-aviv*, or the month of spring. The Hebrew root for the word *Nisan* comes from the Hebrew word for miracles, *nissim*.

Interestingly, the word *Nisan* begins with the Hebrew letter *nun* and ends with the letter *nun*. As one rabbi observed, "Two *nuns* denote *nisei nissim*: many, many miracles. In the era of *Mashiach* [Messiah], everyone will witness great wonders and miracles."[2]

John chapter 2 supports that Yeshua did His first miracle of changing the water into wine in the month of *Nisan*. Then following that miracle, the Bible says, "After this *Yeshua* went down to Capernaum with His mother, brothers, and disciples, and they stayed there a few days. The Jewish feast of Passover was near, so *Yeshua* went up to Jerusalem" (John 2:12–13). Yeshua went up to Jerusalem. Think about that for a moment. He attended the wedding and performed the miracle first. He did His first miracle at the beginning of the month of miracles, *Nisan*.

## Why a Wedding?

John 2:1–3 tells us, "On the third day, there was a wedding at Cana in the Galilee. *Yeshua's* mother was there, and *Yeshua* and His disciples were also invited to the wedding. When the wine ran out, *Yeshua's* mother said to Him, 'They don't have any wine!'"

At first Yeshua was reluctant to be involved. But He chose to help a couple save face, and also launch His ministry there with His first public miracle. To understand why He chose a wedding, we need to dig a bit deeper into God's unique relationship with His people.

### God's Marriage to His People

We must begin by asking, Why was the first miracle done at a wedding? Throughout Scripture, God's relationship with His people is often symbolized spiritually and prophetically, as God being married to His people. God is the groom. Israel is the bride. Ezekiel 16:8 says, "'Again I passed by and saw you, and behold, you were truly at the time of love. I spread the corner of my garment over you and covered your nakedness. I swore to you and entered into a covenant with you,' says ADONAI. 'So you became Mine.'"

Doesn't this remind you of the covenant vows of marriage?

In medieval France and in North Africa, it was common for the groom to place his *tallit* [prayer shawl] over the bride's head to symbolize that he would shelter and protect her. The origin of this custom is found in Ruth's (3:9) words to Boaz, "Spread your robe over your handmaid, for you are a redeeming kinsman"; and, in fact, during the biblical era, such an act constituted a formal betrothal.[3]

Later, German Jews based this practice on a verse from Ezekiel (16:8): "Your time for love had arrived. So I spread my robe over you."[4]

Isaiah 62:4–5 keeps the same theme. The prophet wrote:

No longer will you be termed "Forsaken," no longer your land termed "Desolate." Instead you will be called, "My Delight is in Her" and your land, "Married." For ADONAI delights in you, and your land will be married. For as a young man marries a virgin, so your sons will marry you. As a bridegroom rejoices over a bride, so your God will rejoice over you.

Isaiah was prophesying about marriage to the land but also included God's marriage to His people, writing that He will rejoice over His people as a groom rejoices over his bride on his wedding day. What a beautiful image! I never can forget my own wedding, watching my stunning bride, Miriam, walking toward me. Our eyes were locked, and with each step she took closer to me, my heart rate increased. This is how Yeshua feels toward His bride—us.

God married Israel, but Israel committed spiritual adultery and became estranged from Him. That adultery, the pain of betrayal, broke His heart. Yet, with unfathomable love and faithfulness, the Lord God is constantly calling His bride back to Him (Isa. 54:5–8).

The marriage imagery of God to His people in the Old Testament is evident in Yeshua's first miracle at a wedding. This miracle was a prophetic sign of the coming messianic wedding that we will celebrate with Yeshua, our Bridegroom, in the Kingdom. Yeshua, Israel's Bridegroom. It's symbolic of God saying, *I'm going to reward you and bring you to Me as My wife.*

This time, however, the bride is not just Israel. She may be first and foremost Israel, but not only Israel. The bride of Messiah will include Israel and the nations—one bride who joined themselves to the God of Israel, through Yeshua. Jew and Gentile become one in Messiah, just as Adam and Eve were created to be one.

## Jesus the Bridegroom

The miracle at the wedding was officially the start of Yeshua's public ministry. God was beginning to fulfill the messianic promises, setting His redemption plan into motion. It makes sense that this miracle of abundance occurred at a wedding because Yeshua is the Bridegroom, and He was coming for His bride. The Gospel of John underscores this point:

> John [the Baptist] answered, "A man can receive nothing unless it has been given to him from heaven. You yourselves testify that I said, 'I am not the Messiah,' but rather, 'I am sent before Him.' The one who has the bride is the bridegroom, but the best man rejoices when he stands and hears the bridegroom's voice. So now my joy is complete!" (3:27–29)

Why was John's joy complete? Because he was a humble man who knew what God had called him to do. John also knew it was Yeshua's voice that carried the message that is calling you and me into an intimate relationship with Him. Why is this important? Because it's the voice of Yeshua the Bridegroom that leads us to experience abundance and blessings.

## Provision of Abundance and Blessing

Exodus 21:10 says, "If he marries another woman, he must not deprive the first one of her food, clothing and marital rights" (NIV). This verse points to the threefold biblical obligations of a husband to his wife—sustenance, clothing, and intimate relationship. These are the things God wants to provide for you when you're married to Him. Ultimately, we will see how He fulfills these things in the messianic Kingdom through Yeshua in better and more intimate ways.

Hosea 2:19–20 says, "I will betroth you to me forever; I will betroth you in righteousness and justice, in love and compassion. I will betroth you in faithfulness, and you will acknowledge the LORD" (NIV).

God wants to be your betrothed. Yeshua performed His first miracle at a wedding feast as a sneak preview of the ultimate wedding celebration, the messianic wedding supper of the Lamb, spoken of by the prophets and in the book of Revelation. Revelation 19:7–8 says, "'Let us rejoice and be glad and give him glory! For the wedding of the Lamb has come, and his bride has made herself ready. Fine linen, bright and clean, was given her to wear.' (Fine linen stands for the righteous acts of God's holy people)" (NIV). The wedding in Cana of Galilee points spiritually and prophetically to the type of relationship He wants to have with us.

# The Secret of the Third Day

The story of this miracle opens with the words, *"On the third day*, there was a wedding at Cana in the Galilee." The third day of the week is significant in Jewish wedding traditions. In fact, there are three parts to the Jewish wedding: the *shiddukhin* (arrangements made before the legal betrothal), *erusin* (the betrothal, also known as the period of *kiddushin*—a period of sanctification or being "set apart"), and *nissuin* (marriage).

Many Jewish people are married on the third day. If you are in Israel on the third day of the week, you're going to see many weddings taking place. The reason it's traditional is that the third day is the only day in the Creation account that God blessed twice. Doubly blessed, the third day of the week is Tuesday, and it's considered an auspicious day for weddings because "God saw that it was good" (Gen. 1:10, 12).

These weddings are often held outside in the evening, under the stars. The idea is to symbolize abundance and fruitfulness of your descendants, as God promised that Abraham's descendants would be like the stars of the sky (Gen. 22:17). The Lord brought Abram out into the crisp desert night where the stars were shimmering like billions of diamonds against the blanket of a perfectly dark sky. Oh, what a sight that must have been—no city lights to dim the view! "'Look up now, at the sky, and count the stars—if you are able to count them.' Then He said to him, 'So shall your seed be'" (Gen. 15:5). Those descendants would eventually be from the seed of Yeshua, which includes you and me!

How does this miracle of abundance come? It comes from a relationship with the Messiah, the Bridegroom. He wants you to be doubly blessed. He wants to give you the double portion. He did his first miracle on the third day, which is a day that's doubly good.

The third day is not only connected to double blessing and abundance. It's also connected to revelation at Mount Sinai, where there were three days of preparation to meet God (Ex. 19:15–17).

On the third day, when God revealed Himself as the Bridegroom at Mount Sinai, He came down and gave the Children of Israel the Ten Commandments and ultimately the Torah. This event was a wedding. God married His people on Mount Sinai on the third day.

There's a canopy called a *huppah* at a traditional Jewish wedding. The covering of the canopy is held up by four poles, like a four-post canopy bed. These covers might be quilted and decorated with Jewish symbols like Stars of David or other Judaica art such as a burning bush or olive tree. Often, it is a large prayer shawl, a family *tallit*, or even a family-heirloom tablecloth. The couple stands under the *huppah*, which symbolizes that they're standing under God. He is their covering and the foundation of their family. When God appeared at Mount Sinai, thick clouds hovered over the mountain. The somewhat sagging middle of the *huppah* reminds us of the clouds over Sinai. The image of the bride and groom standing under the *huppah* is also a picture of Israel standing under cloud cover at Mount Sinai.

Moses was a matchmaker. He led the people to Mount Sinai as the bride is led to the groom in the wedding ceremony. A Jewish wedding features a *ketubah*, the wedding contract with the stipulations for the covenant relationship. The Ten Commandments were the *ketubah* for Israel and God.

Also, at the Jewish wedding, the bride circles the groom either three or seven times while he stands under the *huppah*. For the bride, that circling represents that the groom has become the center of her life and world. The deeper symbolism of the bride going around the groom is that God needs to be the one around whom our lives revolve. This is what the Lord was asking of Israel at Sinai and still desires and expects from each of us.

## The Commandment Connection

We can't overlook the connection of the Ten Commandments to a wedding and subsequent marriage. After the three days of preparation on Mount Sinai, God gave the Ten Commandments written by His finger on two tablets of stone. The first tablet contained the commandments between God and man (we are to love the Lord our God). The second one held the commandments between man and man (we are to love our neighbor). Every commandment on the first tablet has a corresponding commandment on the second tablet. Numerically, there's a connection between one and six, and two and seven, three and eight, and so forth. Consider commandments two and seven. The second commandment is "You shall have no other gods before Me" (Ex. 20:3). It pertains to our relationship with God—we shall have no other gods. The seventh commandment is on the second tablet, "Do not commit adultery" (Ex. 20:14). These two commandments connect because both relationships are built on trust and mutual commitment. If a person remains faithful to God, they will likely remain faithful to their spouse. If a person commits spiritual adultery, they are more susceptible to marital infidelity.

Suppose a person does not maintain fidelity to their spouse. In that case, they begin going down a slippery road of idolatry—they have an idol in their life. Idolatry is the equivalent of spiritual adultery. Unfaithfulness violates the covenant relationship—the marriage relationship we have with our spouse is built on, modeled after, and founded on the covenant relationship God establishes with us. After all, He is the husband, and we are the bride. God hates divorce (Mal. 2:16). Divorce results in broken relationships that shatter people's lives. However, God can bring healing.

God unconditionally loves Israel even in their adultery! He's forever calling them back. It's the same love Yeshua embodies as He calls His bride, the church, back to Him. This kind of love is connected to the number 3, which in Jewish numerical thought means redemption, restoration, and resurrection (Hos. 6:2).

This leads us back to Yeshua's wedding miracle. Changing the water to wine on the third day points to Yeshua's resurrection on the third day after His crucifixion. It's on the third day that Yeshua restores us. Subsequently, the first miracle in the book of John connects to the last miracle in the book of John, which is the resurrection. And Yeshua's resurrection ultimately brings us to that greater intimacy with Him.

## Why Is Changing the Water into Wine Jesus' First Miracle?

The changing of water to wine connects to an earlier supernatural sign in the book of Exodus:

> This is what ADONAI says: "By this you will know that I am ADONAI. Behold, I will strike the waters that are in the river with the staff that is in my hand, and they will be turned to blood. The fish that are in the river will die, the river will become foul, and the Egyptians will hate to drink water from the Nile." (Ex. 7:17–18)

Yeshua's first miracle of turning the water into wine showed that He was greater than Moses. This comparison is one of the major themes of the book of John. It shows that Yeshua is the promised messianic Prophet, the second Redeemer, like Moses.

Two things made Moses unique. First, he knew God "face to face" (Deut. 34:10–12) and met Him personally. The Gospel of John begins with "In the beginning was the Word and the Word was face-to-face with God" (author's paraphrase). No one has seen God at any time (John 1:18), but the One who is in the bosom of the Father has made Him known.

John went on to write, "The Word became flesh and tabernacled [dwelled] among us. We looked upon His glory, the glory of the one and only from the Father, full of grace and truth" (John 1:14). The apostle John was showing that Yeshua has an even greater relationship with the Father than Moses did.

Second, Moses was unique in the signs and wonders he performed. Yes, Moses turned water into blood, but Yeshua turned water into wine because He came so that we could have life and have it abundantly (John 10:10).

## Wine: The Sign and Symbol of the Messianic Kingdom

Let's look at what else wine symbolizes in the Old Testament. The rabbis tell us that the following passage from Genesis is speaking about the Messiah:

> The scepter will not pass from Judah, nor the ruler's staff from between his feet, until he to whom it belongs will come. To him will be the obedience of the peoples. Binding his foal to the vine, his donkey's colt to the choice vine, he washes his garments in wine, and in the blood of grapes his robe. His eyes are darker than wine, and teeth that are whiter than milk. (49:10–12)

This verse gives us a vivid picture of Him washing His garments in wine, a symbol of abundance (Amos 9:11).

Jewish holidays and life events are celebrated with wine. This was certainly the case in my home growing up. It was common to have what is called a *kiddush*, a blessing or toast recited over wine before meals on *Shabbat*, holidays, and special occasions such as weddings. In Jewish thought, wine symbolizes joy and abundance. Yeshua's first miracle provided joy and points to the blessing of plenty. This is where He wants us to live—because Yeshua brought kingdom blessing to earth. He died on the cross, giving us restoration, hope, and abundance.

## Wine and the Garden of Eden

Traditionally, the Tree of Knowledge of Good and Evil has been thought of as the apple tree. The idea came from the Song of Solomon. But many rabbis associate the tree with grapes and wine. No other fruit causes as many problems and heartaches as grapes, which are used to make wine. People can drink too much wine and become intoxicated. Rabbis believe that after Noah left the ark, he planted a vineyard to correct the sin of Adam and Eve for eating the forbidden fruit. But Noah failed and gave in to his physical urges and got drunk. It is like a second fall of man, from a biblical and rabbinical understanding of the text.[5]

## Wine and God's Design

Another reason wine is so symbolic of the Kingdom and the Messiah and is featured at Jewish weddings, *Shabbat* (Sabbath), and holidays is because wine is an allusion to God's original design and plan for humanity. God designed us to become wiser and better with time, like good wine. As the wine matures, its texture, quality, taste, richness, and depth only improve. Each time we drink it, we can reflect on the Garden of Eden and God's original intention for humanity. Wine also points to the promise that is coming—a day when the Kingdom will be a reality and death will be no more. We will live forever and, like wine, only mature and become finer with time. Wine represents unlimited potential for blessing, growth, and life. According to the prophet Micah, the symbol of the Kingdom's prosperity and peace is each man sitting under his vine and under his fig tree, "with no one causing terror, for the mouth of *ADONAI-Tzva'ot* [Lord of Hosts] has spoken" (Mic. 4:4). We also find this truth stated in the writings of Zechariah (3:10). Again, we see how wine that comes from the vine points to the messianic Kingdom and to abundance and prosperity.

Wine is a perfect symbol of eternal life because almost every other food decays and worsens over time. Bread gets stale, fruit rots, and, unless it's aged correctly, meat decays. But wine gets better, pointing to the divine design. God wants you to live out of abundance. He's called you to abundant life (John 10:10).

## Living the Abundant Life

Living the John 10:10 life is an extraordinary adventure with the Lord. Deuteronomy 30:19 reminds us that we can choose "between life and death, between blessings and curses . . . Oh, that you would choose life!" (NLT). Yeshua made what some call a "holy interruption." He came. We need to live each day with an attitude of blessing, abundance, and joy. Are you willing to receive the life Yeshua came to give you? You can have it. Abundant life is yours to receive. Just as the wedding guests received the best wine, you can receive the best, most abundant life. How? Keep reading, and let's find out.

### Abundant Faith and Trust

Let's continue with the story of this miracle in John 2:

On the third day, there was a wedding at Cana in the Galilee. *Yeshua's* mother was there, and *Yeshua* and His disciples were also invited to the wedding. When the wine ran out, *Yeshua's* mother said to Him, "They don't have any wine!" *Yeshua* said to her, "Woman, what does this have to do with you and Me? My hour hasn't come yet." His mother said to the servants, "Do whatever He tells you." (vv. 1–5)

Mary (Miriam, in Hebrew) approached Yeshua in faith. She came to Him expecting that He would act on her behalf. Yeshua said, essentially, "Mom, what does this have to do with Me? My hour hasn't arrived." He was telling her it wasn't time for Him to reveal His divine messianic identity and mission. But His mom wouldn't take no for an answer. He was a good Jewish boy, and Jewish boys and their moms have special connections. Yeshua may have remembered the fifth commandment, "Honor your father and mother."

Notice that the miracle didn't happen until the wine ran out. Can you imagine how humiliated and embarrassed the bride's parents must have been? They were responsible for providing for the wedding guests, and they had fallen woefully short. This was a serious miscalculation. The pots were empty, putting a significant kink in the celebration. "How could we let this happen?" they must have been saying. We can tell how concerned Mary was when she saw what was happening. "They don't have any wine!" she exclaimed to Yeshua. The implication was, "Do something!" The wedding planners were in crisis mode. Many times in our lives, we come to a point where there's nothing left. We're emotionally, physically, and monetarily dried up. Often, it's because we've messed up, or someone else has, and it's affecting us. There's been a significant miscalculation in life. When we hit bottom and things dry up, we tend to panic. *I messed up. How could this happen? What am I going to do now? How am I going to make it?* But we need not fear, because God is in control. In fact, He often waits for everything in our lives to run out. I know that sounds harsh, but God allows our own resources to run out so we will run to Him, and He can move us from fear to faith.

There have been many times when our ministry, Fusion Global, has been down financially and we didn't know how we would stay afloat. We are dependent on gifts from people to support what we do. I remember times when I was tempted to freak out, yet God's grace empowered us to stay steady and trust Him for provision. And He's always provided, sometimes in miraculous ways. One time, God called us to be part of a large stadium event in Detroit. We didn't have the money to go, but God said to our spirits, *Go anyway.* We spent $5,000 to get there. It was a complete leap of faith. While we were there, we met a new friend who was led by the Lord to support us. Without knowing what we spent, she gave us a $5,000 check. Her generosity was a sign of God's faithfulness. God says, *I'll provide; just trust Me, and don't live from the place of fear.*

When everything is running out and life is going crazy, the question is, Are you going to choose to see God in it and believe Him for the good? Or are you going to choose to be like Chicken Little and run around like the sky is falling? Faith is about sight, and God wants you to see differently. Helen Keller said, "The worst thing in the world is not to be born blind, but to be born with sight, and yet have no vision."[6]

There is a subtle difference between faith and trust. Faith believes God exists and oversees all Creation, guiding us with His providential hand. Alternatively, trust is acting on our faith. It's stepping out with the confidence that God's got our backs and will provide when we need Him to. It's moving forward knowing He will make a way where there seems to be no way. Trust is faith in action. Mary had both faith and trust when she asked her Son to help at the wedding. If you want to live from a place of abundance, you'll need both. Author and pastor William Barclay wrote, "In every life come periods of darkness when we do not see the way. In every life come things which are such that we do not see why they came or any meaning in them. Happy are those who in such a case still trust even when they cannot understand."[7]

## Abundant Obedience

In God's terms, living in abundance is living in obedience. Mary told the servants, "Do whatever He tells you" (John 2:5). In our culture, obedience has become negative and unsatisfying, while cynicism and unbelief are seen as cool. Unfortunately, the current culture has it wrong. To disobey God dismisses the blessing. It goes back to the Garden of Eden. Adam and Eve disbelieved, and it led to their disobedience. They ate from the tree, and they were dismissed from the Garden and all its blessings. Belief and trust lead to abundance. It's simple: do what God says in His Word. Don't delay. If you wait or procrastinate on what God tells you to do, you're being disobedient, plain and simple. Author Jessica LaGrone wrote, "In India, children are taught, 'Slow obedience is no obedience.'"[8]

## Abundant *Chutzpah*

*Chutzpah* is a Yiddish word that means "nerve"[9] or "holy audacity." I can just picture a stout Jewish woman in 1940s Germany with her hands planted firmly on her hips saying, "Rubbish!" when replying to orders from Nazi soldiers. Corrie ten Boom showed *chutzpah* when she hid Jews in her home during the Holocaust. But it's more than holy backbone. Mary, when saying, "Do whatever He tells you," taught us that we cannot accomplish anything great without faith and *chutzpah*.

There's a good aspect and a bad aspect to *chutzpah*. The bad is stubbornly refusing to let go of your own plan; yet, if you're going to do anything extraordinary for God, you must have shameless boldness and obedience. You need *chutzpah*. It is the antithesis to and the antidote for fear. An audacious spiritual nerve in the best sense, *chutzpah* is about having the faith to stand firm when necessary and to move forward and take risks for God when led. Mary wasn't going to take no for an answer when she talked to Jesus at the wedding in Cana. She was willing to risk everything because of her faith. Faith is spelled R-I-S-K. Having faith will embolden us to take risks.

Yeshua is one of the greatest examples of holy *chutzpah*. At the end of John 2, we read about how He went into the Temple and overturned the tables of the money changers. That took *chutzpah*. If we're going to do extraordinary things for God, we can't be passive. We can't be timid, fearful, or intimidated. Moses told the people to choose which way they wanted to live (Deut. 30:19). I choose to nurture this characteristic because I know that I can never fully serve God or walk in my destiny apart from holy *chutzpah*.

Habakkuk 2:4 reminds us, "the righteous one will live by his faith" (NASB). God is looking for people who in the difficult times are willing to stand with an abundance of *chutzpah* that is rooted in faith and trust, and who won't take no for an answer. What about you? Do you need a shot of *chutzpah*?

## The Secret of the Six Stone Pots

When reading about this miracle in John's gospel, we need to be alert to its symbolism, which provides deeper messianic secrets to explore. These symbols offer a broader understanding of what God wants us to know, directly impacting our faith and life as believers in Messiah. The stone pots at the Cana wedding are a profound example of this, especially that there were six of them. In Jewish thought,

- Six is the number of creation. God worked for six days, then rested on the seventh.
- Six is the number of man. God created the first man and woman, Adam and Eve, on the sixth day of creation.
- Man fell on the sixth day; he ate from the tree on the sixth day.

Yeshua's first miracle involved six stone pots because He came as both the Second Adam[10] and the Savior. Since the Fall happened on the sixth day, the Messiah died on the sixth day, which on the Hebrew calendar is Friday. What makes Good Friday so good is that the Messiah came to restore what we lost in Eden. Not only did the Messiah die on the sixth day, He was also on the cross for six hours and was even pierced in six places:

- His head was pierced with a crown of thorns (John 19:2).
- His side was pierced (John 19:32–35).
- His two hands were pierced (fulfilling Psalm 22:16).
- His two feet were pierced (fulfilling Psalm 22:16).

## The Sign of Restoring the Connection

The significance of the number 6 goes even further. The letter *vav* [ו] is the sixth letter of the Hebrew alphabet. It's written in the shape of a man and is the most used letter in the Torah. Nearly every verse in the Torah begins with a *vav* since it connects one verse to another. In Genesis 1:1, the sixth Hebrew word begins with a *vav*—connecting heaven and (*vav*) earth. When we sinned, we broke the connection between heaven and earth. Yeshua came to restore the connection between heaven and earth. He died on the cross to restore that connection, so abundance and blessing can flow into our lives in greater measure once again.

There's yet another connection with the number 6 we should consider. This connection is not a restoration but a look forward. The rabbis teach us it is "the wine that has been preserved in its grapes since the six days of creation."[11] There's good wine in the grapes that come from the Garden of Eden and from the six days of Creation. The six stone pots point to the wine that has been preserved since those six days of Creation. Yeshua was giving the guests at the wedding at Cana a taste of the marriage supper of the Lamb, when the good wine would be served. It was a sneak preview of the abundant life to come.

## New Old Wine

Another integral part of this miracle is that Yeshua created a curious combination: new old wine. The wine was brand-new but tasted old. This shows that God can take something that is new and supernaturally mature it. He did it to wine, and He can do it to you, giving depth and ability beyond your years of knowledge, experience, and skill. It's supernatural maturation. But the combination of new and old is also symbolic of the Kingdom. It's symbolic of Jew and Gentile coming together. Yeshua said, "Every scribe instructed concerning the kingdom of heaven is like a householder who brings out of his treasure things new and old" (Matt. 13:52 NKJV).

Hidden treasures are both old and new. If you rummage through your storage room or closet, you'll likely find that you have new and old items you treasure. What we often miss is the blessing when we bring both together. Maybe an old Bible with a new commentary. Or, more importantly, the truths of the Old Testament brought together with the truth of the New Testament. Spiritual truth is the greatest treasure because it transforms us and our relationship with the Lord. Seeing these connections between the Old and the New renews and strengthens our faith and gives us a sense of wonder and deeper love for God's Word. The miracle of the new old wine points to the incredible things that happen when new and old are joined.

## Expect the Unexpected

This miracle of water into wine illustrates that God wants to show up in counterintuitive ways. We need to expect the unexpected. He transformed the water into wine partly because water is ordinary and wine is extraordinary. Turning the water into wine reflects the promise that God takes the ordinary and turns it into something extraordinary. He's a God who wants to bless us. He wants us to live in abundance. It's an extraordinary transformation that we can personally experience. That's why 2 Corinthians 5:17 tells us that if any are in the Messiah, they are a new creation. The old has gone, and the new is here. The old is passing away, and the new, the extraordinary life of abundance, is coming.

God doesn't want you to live out of the lack. He wants you to live out of the overflow. Make no mistake: His blessings are abundant and extravagant. "They filled them [the pots] to the brim" (John 2:7 NIV). God wants you to live life to the brim. He wants you to overflow with blessing and abundance. But it takes faith, trust, obedience, and *chutzpah*. Think about this for a moment. Those stone pots were heavy! Each one held around twenty gallons. The servants had to lug them outside to the water source and fill them up, which took time. I can picture the servants mumbling to each other, "This is nuts. What are we doing? The guests don't want water. They want wine. They are expecting wine." Yet they did it. Think of the obedience that took, simply at Yeshua's word, as Mary told them. "Do whatever He tells you." She expected a miracle. When you walk in obedience, no matter how unreasonable it may seem at times, you live in the overflow and can expect miracles. Expect that the best is yet to come. This is one of the secrets to living the abundant life.

# TWO

# THE SIGNS AND SECRETS
# OF PURIFICATION

I love Passover. It's foundational to every part of Jewish life. What's interesting is that the remembrance of the miracle of the exodus from Egypt is the foundation of all Jewish holidays, and who doesn't love a good holiday celebrating miracles?

We've established that *Nisan* is the Hebrew month of miracles. It is also the month of the Passover, in which God delivered the Children of Israel out of Egypt. During the Passover season, it's rewarding to look at some of the miracles and mysteries of the Messiah. These are not all obvious miracles, but they have signs and mysteries connected to them that prompt the supernatural in our own lives.

## The Process of Transformation

The miracle of turning water into wine was the first sign of Yeshua (John 2:1–12). It was a miracle of blessing, abundance, and transformation.

God transformed something ordinary into something extraordinary, just as He does with us when He touches our lives and transforms us into new creations. We are turned from water into wine. The old passes away, and the new comes. However, this transformation is not a one-and-done thing but rather a lifetime process of becoming. Personally, I am being transformed daily from something ordinary into something extraordinary. The old is passing away, and the new is coming into my life. I'm excited as I witness the things God is doing in me. And I'm convinced He wants to do it in your life too.

A key aspect of transformation is purification. There is a purging of the old to usher in the new you. Purification, as a part of transformation, leads to freedom.

God redeemed the Children of Israel out of Egypt at Passover, and the miracle of water into wine took place around Passover. Passover is about redemption, but redemption is not complete without transformation and purification. God brought Israel out of Egypt, but He had to take Egypt out of Israel. This purging is what leads to true freedom. Therefore, we see Yeshua in John 2 purging the Temple in Jerusalem.

## Overturning the Tables

Near Passover Jesus went to Jerusalem. John 2:14–16 tells us:

> In the Temple area he saw merchants selling cattle, sheep, and doves for sacrifices; he also saw dealers at tables exchanging foreign money. Jesus made a whip from some ropes and chased them all out of the Temple. He drove out the sheep and cattle, scattered the money

changers' coins over the floor, and turned over their tables. Then, going over to the people who sold doves, he told them, "Get these things out of here. Stop turning my Father's house into a marketplace!" (NLT)

As we stated earlier, Yeshua showed some *chutzpah* here. We must ask, Why did He drive out the money changers, right after He performed the miracle of the water into wine, as His second public act? What is the spiritual meaning and significance? The key to understanding all this is remembering that the context is Passover, a holiday known as *Zman Cheiruteinu* in Hebrew. *Zman* means "time," and *Cheiruteinu* means "freedom"; it is the "time of our freedom." God told Moses to go to Pharaoh and say, "Let My people go, so *they may serve Me*" (Ex. 7:16, 26; 9:1, 13; 10:3, emphasis mine). God's not out to get you but to free you. Freedom, however, leads to serving Him. If you are in bondage, you will never serve the Lord and fulfill your divine purpose. Ask yourself: In what way am I choosing to live in slavery (former sins, addiction, unforgiveness, etc.)? And why?

We are called to worship and serve God, but it must be done in purity. We need to be purified. That's part of the process—redemption is supplied, but then it must be applied through the sanctification, purification, and the purging of the old nature of the old man. During some of my most difficult seasons, when my calling seemed to be delayed and it looked like it would never happen, God worked on many levels. One was purging Jason of Jason. We can fall into the trap of pride, or remain fearful, but God works in and through us. Remember, delays are not denials. They usually mean God is working on something in us or preparing the way for our destiny.

## Removing the Leaven

Another way to say this is that we are removing the leaven from our lives. Often Scripture uses leaven, or the rising agent in bread, as a symbol of sin. It's critical to our understanding of the Passover, especially the tradition in which all leaven is removed from Jewish homes. It's also a key to grasping why Yeshua overturned the money changers' tables when He was in Jerusalem celebrating Passover. The Scriptures declare, "For seven days you are to eat *matzot* [unleavened bread], but on the first day you must remove *hametz* [leaven or foods containing leaven] from your houses, for whoever eats *hametz* from the first day until the seventh day, that soul will be cut off from Israel" (Ex. 12:15). The first day of this holiday with unleavened bread is Passover, but the rest of the seven-day period is called *Chag HaMatzot*, or the Feast of Unleavened Bread. There was no leaven found in the Children of Israel's houses, which is true even today.

For several days or weeks before the Passover, the Orthodox Jewish family begins to clean the house from top to bottom. Every crevice and corner is vacuumed and cleaned to make sure the *hametz* is removed. They open every book and ensure there are no bread crumbs in it. They move every pillow on the couch, search their car, and check their cupboards. There is an intricate process, known as *kashering* or "koshering," to make the home kosher and fit for Passover. Some people use separate dishes and flatware that have never had leaven on them, and I've even taken a blowtorch to metal pans! They must clean the counters thoroughly, maybe with boiling water or an iron, or some people cover their counters with aluminum foil. This is an elaborate operation that is the primary preparation for Passover.[1]

It also means removing all products that contain leavening agents.

The evening before Passover begins, the parents hide about ten pieces of leaven in the home. The children take a wooden spoon (miniature dustpan), a feather (tiny broom), a napkin, and either a candle (from an ancient Jewish custom) or a flashlight, and they search for the leaven in the home.[2] The next day it is traditional to burn all the leaven in the morning. We also speak the phrase "All the *hametz*, all the leaven, and leavened bread in my possession, which I have not seen and do not remove, as well as any that I am not aware of, is null and ownerless as the dust of the earth."

The biblical holidays are not meant to be rote, mindless rituals. Rather, the Jewish people embrace these annual rhythms as opportunities to not only worship God but to do so as a family. These "appointed times" (Lev. 23:1–4) are also memorable ones!

One of my favorite traditions involves the search for ten pieces of leavened bread that I mentioned earlier. These pieces of leaven are hidden around the home for the kids to find. As they search from room to room, we usually help them by telling them they are "hot" or "cold."

During one memorable experience, my kids were searching for an unusually long time. No leavened bread could be found. After they complained, I decided to check a few spots where we hid the bread. I knew I was good at hiding things but not *that* good. Having pored over the entire house, I finally discovered that we weren't the only ones searching for the hidden unleavened bread. Another party had discovered it before us (and enjoyed it immensely): our golden retriever, Sammy!

While that was a funny experience, these traditions exist to remind us of something quite important. We need to remember that the preparation for Passover connects directly with what Yeshua did with the money changers in the Temple. Understanding the tradition of removing the leaven from the home and the process that accompanies it is important because it helps us understand that Yeshua overturned the tables of the money changers as a faithful Son to cleanse His Father's house, the Temple, in preparation for the Passover.

What are the reasons for the elaborate spring cleaning and the removal of the leaven? First, it reminds us that the Israelites left Egypt in great haste, and they ate unleavened bread (Ex. 12:33–34). We eat it to remind us of the speedy redemption. It is known as the bread of redemption or the bread of affliction because it reminds us of slavery in Egypt. It's broken, which reminds us of the cruelty and harsh labor we endured in Egypt.

Second, leaven is also symbolic of sin in the Bible and Jewish tradition. "'Watch out,' *Yeshua* said to them, 'and beware of the *hametz* [leaven] of the Pharisees and Sadducees'" (Matt. 16:6). Rabbi Alexandri, a famous rabbi, would end his prayers with the following supplication: "Master of the Universe, You know full well that it is our desire to act according to Your will, but what prevents us? The yeast in the dough."[3] In Jewish mystical traditions, man's evil inclination, his sin nature, is called the leaven in the dough. Just as yeast is put in the dough and makes it ferment and become *hametz*, or leavened, the evil inclination in man is what entices and puffs us up to sin. In Jewish thought, *hametz* symbolizes the evil inclination.

The blessed and holy One said,

All those years a foreign nation, Egypt, enslaved you, and forces of Egypt controlled you. Now, though, you are free, for I have lifted you from the bondage. When the Torah states, Remove the leaven from your home, you should not eat anything that is leaven, and leaven shall not be seen in your possession—it hints that Pesach [the Paschal Lamb] matzah stand for freedom from the forces of evil [the world, the flesh, Satan] which hametz symbolize.[4]

That is why Passover is the festival of redemption and freedom, when we carefully seek to rid ourselves of the *hametz* and evil inclination. Specifically, *hametz* is associated with three sins: jealousy, the thirst for physical pleasures, and the hunger for honor. We want to be the *matzah*, not the *hametz*. To purge the leaven of idols and false religious beliefs—the lies we believe about God, others, and ourselves. The word *pharaoh* means "mouth of evil."[5] We were enslaved in Egypt by evil speech, and part of freedom is coming out of agreement with these lies, false beliefs, and idols that we've made substitutes for God. God wants to rid us of all these things. He wants to purify us and purge these things from us, not wanting us to live with the leaven.

## Burning the Leaven

There are two aspects of Passover. The first is called Passover, commemorating how the Lord spared the Children of Israel from the death of the firstborn, and the other is the companion seven-day feast, the Feast of Matzah, in which we are removing the leaven, being transformed as we remove all those unhealthy things from our lives. We are coming out from under the power of the pharaoh of the world, the flesh, and the devil. *Egypt* for us stands for a place of gross materialism in perverted form, symbolized by the leaven. When we break down the Hebrew word for Passover, *Pesach*, into two words, *pes* means "annulment," and *chet* is "sin." It is the removal of sin. We see this removal in the burning of the leaven, which represents the removal of sin not just from the Temple but from our lives.

On the morning before Passover, the family—or just the children—searches the house for leaven that has been hidden. When it is all discovered, it's stored in a safe place. A special fire is made to burn the leaven, accompanied by a special blessing.[6]

When we consider this miracle of purification Yeshua performed in John 2, we must remember that He did it again. He cleared the Temple twice. Yeshua bookends His ministry with acts of removing the spiritual leaven from His Father's house in preparation for the Passover. Yeshua's first recorded public act is in John 2 when He purified the Temple. In Matthew 21 He did the same thing, after riding into Jerusalem on a donkey on Palm Sunday. He purified His Father's house before the last Passover He celebrated on the earth—the Seder (Passover meal) with His disciples—overturning the tables of the money changers a second time. Yeshua comes to bring the fire that burns leaven from our lives.

Yeshua said the rejection of Him would lead to the destruction of God's house, and it would be destroyed by fire. It is the fire that brings judgment. It is the fire of purification. The fire that burns the leaven. Those who refuse Yeshua will receive judgment for the sin in their lives. And even for believers, to the degree that the leaven is not removed in our lives, at the time of the ultimate fulfillment of Passover, the coming of the Messiah, the leaven that is left will be burned. Leaven in your life must be burned. This is not a fire unto salvation but rather tests the quality of how believers have lived their lives. Paul spoke about our works being burned up like stubble, and his comment has nothing to do with our salvation. Our reward is determined by the quality of our works.

The apostle and rabbi Paul wrote:

Now if anyone builds on the foundation with gold, silver, precious stones, wood, hay, straw, each one's work will become clear. For the Day will show it, because it is to be revealed by fire; and the fire itself will test each one's work—what sort it is. If anyone's work built on the foundation survives, he will receive a reward. If anyone's work is burned up, he will suffer loss—he himself will be saved, but as through fire. (1 Cor. 3:12–15)

Our personal Egypts are not merely punishment for disobedience. Exile is part of the process of redemption that leads to new creation and transformation.

## King Josiah and the Passover Revival

We find this concept of removing idolatry and false religious beliefs in 2 Kings 22–24. Some sages point to the story of King Josiah as reason to associate the removal of leaven with the destruction of idols and false religious beliefs (2 Kings 23:21–25).

Josiah was one of the most memorable revival kings of Israel. The Scriptures say that no king like him has arisen since. Josiah did more than bring back the God-ordained Passover holiday. He brought revival to Jerusalem at Passover by removing the idols and false beliefs. We all have things in our lives that keep us enslaved in Egypt that must be purged and released. When they are, it brings personal revival and freedom.

I once had a dream that the Holy Spirit took me to my closet and told me to remove all the clothes, and every time I reached for something, I didn't want to get rid of it. Every piece had special memories associated with it—what I wore for my wedding or what I wore when my son was born. I didn't want to let go. The Lord said, *Jason, I want to give you a new wardrobe. I want to give you an upgrade. But if you want to wear these old clothes, you can't also wear the new ones.* I realized the old clothes represented my old hurts, old ways of seeing, old ways of being, unhealthy relationships, and the unhealthy things from the past that I hung on to. Those clothes weren't going to look good on me—they didn't fit me anymore, and they were out of style. I needed to eliminate the old to make room for the new. I realized there must be displacement before replacement and purging before the promise of the new can come. God said I needed to clean my closet, which is like cleaning the house of the leaven—searching for and removing the leaven of idols, addictions, impurities, unhealthy relationships, and sin from our lives. Removing leaven at Passover reminds us of the need to fight against the influence and control of the world, the flesh, and the devil in our lives and those secret sins and addictions we all have.

The punishment for not removing the leaven during Passover is being cut off, which makes sense because sin separates us and cuts us off from God and His blessings. Scripture teaches us that the soul that sins dies and that our sins have created a barrier between us and the Lord (Isa. 59:1–2). Sin creates barriers and blocks the blessing. All of us have some leaven in our lives, and we need to be more concerned about removing that leaven than pointing out the leaven in others.

## The Sign of Preparing His Father's House

As I mentioned earlier, Yeshua performed the cleansing of the Temple during Passover in John 2, which is the time of freedom, redemption, and purification. This act points to His identity and authority as the Son of God. Every good Jewish child's responsibility is to help his parents, especially his father, prepare the house for Passover. As a kid, preparing for Passover was a big deal around our household. We degreased the oven, sanitized sinks in the kitchen and bathrooms, and cleaned out the fridge and pantries. Nothing remained that had leaven or flour, even cookies and cake! I had to pitch in. While it was work, there was also an air of excitement and significance. Of course, I was still a kid who had his mind on playing and running with my friends. Not so with Yeshua. Even at a young age, He understood what He came into the world to do and that the Temple in Jerusalem was His Father's house.

As a young boy, Yeshua's parents went up to Jerusalem every year for Passover. When He was twelve years old, they went according to the festival custom. When they began the journey home, they didn't realize Yeshua was not with them; He had remained in Jerusalem "sitting in the center of the teachers, listening to them and asking them questions" (Luke 2:46).

They found Yeshua in the Temple because it was His Father in heaven's house. The Temple was the place where God set His presence. This moment showed that Yeshua is the Messiah and the One "greater than Moses" promised by the Torah and the prophets. We've discussed how Jesus was greater than Moses in His miracles and His access to God. And now, Jesus made the connection again in the Temple. Moses dedicated and erected the Tabernacle, the first Temple, in the month of *Nisan*, the month of the Passover. The Temple in Jerusalem was dedicated in the month of *Nisan*. Moses' unique relationship with God was demonstrated by the fact that he could enter the Holy of Holies anytime he wanted, unlike Aaron and other high priests, who could enter only once a year on the Day of Atonement.

Yeshua's cleansing of the Temple at the start of His ministry demonstrated and testified to His unique relationship as God's Son because He was helping His Father prepare the house for Passover. His first miracle of water into wine demonstrated His unique power, but the cleansing of the Temple was the first sign that bore witness to His unique and intimate relationship with the Father. He did it publicly to bring attention to His true identity and authority.

## The Secret Meaning of "Destroy This Temple in Three Days"

Not only did Jesus cleanse the Temple, but directly afterward, He identified with the Temple as His very body. After Jesus overturned the tables and shooed out the moneylenders, Judean leaders were incensed. They came demanding an explanation.

The Judean leaders responded, "What sign do You show us, since You are doing these things?"

> "Destroy this Temple," *Yeshua* answered them, "and in three days I will raise it up." The Judean leaders then said to Him, "Forty-six years this Temple was being built, and You will raise it up in three days?" But He was talking about the temple of His body. So after He was raised from the dead, His disciples remembered that He was talking about this. Then they believed the Scripture and the word that *Yeshua* had spoken. (John 2:18–22)

It's interesting to note that the Judean leaders who knew Scriptures were incensed and yet the disciples—who included uneducated fishermen—"Remembered." The key here is that they remembered the words Yeshua spoke to them. That's an important lesson for us. We can't study the Bible enough. We must live on its foundation. But more than study, it's important that we bring the Bible into our hearts, so we believe and act on our faith in God's Word.

# Yeshua and the Number 2

There's something even deeper here. This was Yeshua's *second* public act. Because Hebrew is alphanumeric, we regard this as especially significant. The number 2 in Hebrew is written with the Hebrew letter *bet* (ב), and the Hebrew letter *bet* means "house" or "house of the father." The Temple in Jerusalem is called *beit hamikdash*, which is "the holy house."

The letter *bet*, the second letter of the Hebrew alphabet, also points to the Son, because the word for son—*ben*—begins with the letter *bet*. The first letter of Genesis 1:1 ("beginning") is *bet* in Hebrew. The last letter of Revelation in Hebrew is *nun*, so the first letter and last letter spell *son*, *BeN*. The Bible is all about the *ben*, Yeshua, the *Son*. The word *ben* also has numerical significance in Hebrew. *Ben* (son) has the numeric value of 2. Father is the number 1; 2 is the letter *bet*, the letter associated with the house where the fullness of God's glorious presence resides because of the incarnation. Yeshua is the second person of the Godhead, the number 2, and He is the *ben*, the Son, and He's also the house.

We can see this all coming together in several places in Scripture. Jewish tradition says the world stands on three pillars: (1) the Torah, the Word of God; (2) sacrifices and worship; and (3) deeds of kindness.[7] The second sign, performed in the house of God, or the *bet*, is connected to the number 2, which represents sacrifice (the second pillar). That is also connected to the Son, who is the second person of the Godhead who offered Himself as the ultimate sacrifice. The Son is the true *bet*. Jesus Himself is the Temple. John the Revelator saw this in his vision:

> I also saw the holy city—the New Jerusalem—coming down out of heaven from God, prepared as a bride adorned for her husband. . . . I

saw no temple in her, for its Temple is *Adonai Elohei-Tzva'ot* and the Lamb. (Rev. 21:2, 22)

The New Jerusalem doesn't have a Temple house. It has Yeshua. He is the true Temple because the presence of God dwells in Him, not in a physical building. His body was God's house. That's the deeper meaning of Yeshua's cleansing of the temple. He said, "Destroy this Temple . . . and in three days I will raise it up" (John 2:19). His body is the new temple in the New Jerusalem.

According to Jewish tradition, God's glory did not dwell in the second Temple, which was the one in which Yeshua worshiped, but according to the New Testament, it dwelled in Yeshua Himself. He was the carrier of God's presence. He was the locus of the *shekinah*, God's manifest glory. John 2:11 tells us Yeshua "revealed His glory" in the first miracle of transforming the water into wine. There are layers of connection here: by killing Him, the leaders destroyed the true *bet*, the house of God, the second person, and the Temple connected to the sacrifice, which, according to Jewish tradition, is the second pillar the world stands on.

## Defeating the Leaven and Evil Inclination

Numbers in the Bible show how precise our God is. Every detail of the universe, down to the microscopic level, is ordered beyond comprehension. So is the Word of God. God is all-knowing and all-powerful, and every one of us has a unique and individual number. It's called DNA. That's how personal God is. The Bible is a living book with a DNA code too.

Let's review what I mentioned earlier. Each Hebrew letter has a corresponding number. Hebrew and Greek, unlike many other languages, don't have a separate number table, so they use letters to represent numbers. To determine a word's numeric value, we simply add the numeric value of the letters. For example, the word we just studied, BeN, has a numeric value of *bet* (2) plus *nun* (50), or 52.

We will uncover quite a bit of numerical meaning in the miracles of Jesus. I realize that all these numbers can be mind-boggling, but stick with me here, and let's discover just how remarkably these symbols tie together.

*Hametz*, which again is the Hebrew word for leaven, has the numerical value of 138 in the Hebrew alphabet. This is significant because this is also the number of the word *tzemach*, which means "branch." "Branch" is one of Messiah's primary names. It is a messianic title in the books of Jeremiah and Zechariah. Jeremiah 33:15 says, "In those days and at that time, I will cause a Branch of Righteousness to spring up for David, and He will execute justice and righteousness in the land." What was happening in the Temple was unjust and unrighteous, and so the Branch (138) had to remove the leaven (138).

Isaiah 9:6 gives us one of the key messianic prophecies: "For to us a child is born, a son will be given to us, and the government will be upon His shoulder. His Name will be called Wonderful Counselor, Mighty God My Father of Eternity, Prince of Peace."

The numerical value of the words "to us a son" is 138, which relates to the letter *bet*, the letter of the Son. The Son (138) who is given to us is the "Branch" (138), who was sent to remove the leaven (138). Interestingly, the Hebrew phrase translated "My servant will prosper" (Isa. 52:13), about the death of the Messiah, also has a numerical value of 138. Even more incredible is that 138 is the mathematical value of the term that translates to "Son of God" (*ben Elohim*). This alludes to the fact that the Son spoken of in Isaiah 9:5 is also the Branch. He is the divine Son of

God (138), who will cause the will of the Lord to prosper (138). And the Lord's prosperity comes from removing the leaven (138) from our lives. It's a precise message worked into the very DNA of the Bible, and one we can all benefit from.

## Celebrating the Mini-Passover

We all have leaven in our lives. Sometimes that leaven is hidden deep within us, but like the children searching from room to room for leaven, we need to search every corner of our hearts and lives to remove it. This shouldn't be limited to the season of Passover. Remember what the apostle Paul said in 1 Corinthians 5:6–8:

> Don't you know that a little *hametz* leavens the whole batch of dough? Get rid of the old *hametz*, so you may be a new batch, just as you are unleavened—for Messiah, our Passover Lamb, has been sacrificed. Therefore let us celebrate the feast not with old *hametz*, the *hametz* of malice and wickedness, but with unleavened bread—the *matzah* of sincerity and truth.

Every time we partake of the Lord's Supper, it is a mini-Passover. Drinking the cup and eating the bread is a most sacred moment when we slow down and reflect on how His body was broken and His blood poured out on the cross for us. It proclaims His death, resurrection, and return! We respond by searching our hearts for any leaven so that we don't partake in an unworthy manner (1 Cor. 11:27–31). The regular partaking of this shows that we are to take an accounting of the soul and search our hearts on a regular basis to remove the leaven.

# The Unification of God's People

We've explored several reasons why it was important that Jesus purified the Temple as His second public act. Yet another important reason it had to be cleansed is that the Temple played a unifying role in uniting God's people. The Jewish people prayed toward Jerusalem, just as Daniel did while in exile (Dan. 6:11). All Jews contributed to its support with the half shekel and were supposed to go up to Jerusalem three times a year to worship for the three pilgrimage holidays—*Pesach* (Passover), *Shavuot* (Weeks or Pentecost), and *Sukkot* (The Feast of Tabernacles, Tents, or Booths). However, the Temple was not just a house of worship for Israel. It was meant to be a house of worship for all nations: "My House will be called a House of Prayer for all nations" (Isa. 56:7).

Jesus had to clear the Temple to make this possible. There were three courts in the temple: the Court of the Gentiles, the Court of the Women, and the Court of Israel. A barricade in the Court of the Women stated no foreigner would enter the forecourt and the balustrade around the sanctuary. Anyone who was caught would have himself to blame for his subsequent death.

Gentiles could go to only one place in the Temple. Because so many pilgrims came during Passover, money changers and vendors who sold sacrifices set up in the Court of the Gentiles for that one week of the year, according to the *Mishnah*, an earlier part of the Jewish writings[8] and in agreement with the opinion of Jewish leader (10 BC to AD 70) Rabban Shimon ben Gamliel.[9] The one place in the Temple where nations (Gentiles) could go worship and pray was turned into a noisy marketplace that was not conducive to worship.

There is a deep, prophetic, messianic aspect to Yeshua's action because, in Zechariah 14:20–21, the prophet spoke of the eschatological renewal of worship, or the way worship will be at the end of days. He said there will no longer be a trader or a merchant in the House of God. Yeshua showed Himself to be the messianic One whom God promised in Zechariah. He was the unique Son of God, the Messiah, the One who was going to fulfill the prophecy. Yeshua's driving out the money changers was a sneak preview of what He will accomplish in the messianic Kingdom.

God desired for Gentiles and Jews to worship together. He wants there to be unity in worship. It's the fusion of Gentile and Jew, of old and new, into one new man. Equality does not equal sameness. Jews don't have to become Gentiles. Gentiles don't have to become Jews. We don't have to worship in the same way, but equality means that there is equal value. As I've written about in other books, I have Gentile friends who were instrumental in my salvation. They helped open my eyes to the truth that Yeshua was the Messiah and opened my eyes to who I really was.

Our worship and our service to God are equally valuable, and there is equal spiritual access to God in worship and prayer. That's why Yeshua rent the veil in two (Matt. 27:51) rather than in four or another number. Now the Holy of Holies, separated by this thick veil or curtain, was open to both Jews and Gentiles. There's a new way for Jews and a new way for Gentiles.

The miracle of Jesus' purification in John 2 showed Gentile mistreatment. The priests didn't show respect for the importance of the worship and prayer of the nations. But it's ultimately through Yeshua, the true Temple, that Israel and the nations are unified. Just as the Temple unified Israel, Yeshua is the Temple that unifies us. The nations connect to Israel and God's promises through the resurrected Yeshua. He is now the center. Just as all Jews pray toward Jerusalem, we pray to Yeshua, not to the Temple. We are unified in Him. God freed Israel so that they would worship Him. It makes sense that this miracle occurred in the context of the temple, the worship, and the Passover. The Temple was to be a place of consecration, not commerce.

## Your Personal Egypt

Leaven and Egypt are connected in the way we celebrate Passover every year. Passover is not merely a remembrance but a present reoccurrence in our lives. Egypt is not just a physical location; it is a spiritual state. All of us have our own personal Egypts, and the journey of coming out of Egypt is a lifelong process. The Hebrew word for Egypt is *Mizraim*, and it means "confinement," "limitation," or "restriction." Egypt was a place of impurity and enslavement for the Children of Israel. It prevented the souls of God's people from understanding and actualizing their true identity and destiny. Egypt is understood as the root of all of Israel's exiles. From the time of the Abrahamic promise and the birth of Isaac, Israel lived as sojourners, as foreigners, in exile until God brought them out of Egypt and gave them the land that He promised to Abraham, Isaac, and Jacob.

Israel, the Promised Land, represents transformation, the New Jerusalem, and the place of promise for our lives. We associate Egypt with leaven, sin, and evil inclinations. The Promised Land is a place where we can break through the confinement and limitations so we can physically and spiritually overcome the evil inclinations in our lives. It symbolizes the place where we can personally and corporately reach our true identities and potential. It is not merely a physical place, but it is a spiritual reality, and it is a Person. Hope is a Person. Love is a Person. Peace is a Person. It is Yeshua. Entering the Promised Land is entering into Yeshua.

That's why Paul wrote that we are "called to *Yeshua* the Messiah" (Rom. 1:6). We enter into Him like Israel entered the Promised Land to find purification and salvation.

When we live in our personal Egypts, we live in a state of exile. Exile is about distance and disconnection on a spiritual, relational, physical, and psychological level. We're not enslaved by people, but we are enslaved by sin. This is the deeper meaning of the phrase God used to tell His people how to celebrate Passover: "You are to tell your son on that day saying, 'It is because of what *ADONAI* did for me when I came out of Egypt'" (Ex. 13:8). In every generation, we are to tell our children, "I came out of Egypt." Though I didn't come out of the country of Egypt, I can celebrate the inner, eternal spiritual meaning of coming out of Egypt as a lifetime process. That's why Passover is *Zman Cheiruteinu*, or "the time of our freedom." We are being freed from exile.

## A Kernel in the Soil

You are a kernel or a seed, and exile is the soil in which the seed breaks open from confinement and grows into a new tree. Have you ever considered the miracle of a seed? Within every kernel is the promise or DNA, the germ of life—of what it will become. When we hold a pack of seeds in our hands, we have a future forest of giant red oaks or a garden of magnificent fruits or vegetables. Yet it must first be buried and die for it to grow and become what it was created to be. Essentially, the seed's original form ceases and transforms into something new. It's born again. How does this happen other than the miraculous power of an all-powerful God? "Unless a grain of wheat falls to the earth and dies, it remains alone. But if it dies, it produces much fruit" (John 12:24). This death of the seed is a little like exile in Egypt. It is necessary. We need exile in the place of struggle and restrictions, because exile is like the dirt in which that seed must die. We must die to the past, to self, and to the leaven of sin. It is in that death that the seed splits open. Redemption is when the seed grows and begins to break through the soil of exile.

But redemption must be preceded by exile. God uses it for the good to transform us. Exile is the preparation. Abraham went into exile in Egypt. Moses went into exile in Egypt. Israel went into exile in Egypt, and even Messiah Yeshua had to go to Egypt as a child and came out of Egypt—the root of all exiles—so He could fulfill His destiny as the Redeemer and the One who was "greater than Moses." So just as Moses instituted Passover and had the people remove the leaven from their homes, so Yeshua removed the leaven from the Temple and celebrated the Passover. This is good news. Yeshua's two cleansings of God's house were prophetic, symbolic acts that He would remove the leaven from our lives because He is the unique Son of God. But we must actively desire and partner with Him for this to become a reality.

Because Yeshua is greater than Moses, who brings about a greater redemption symbolized by turning the water into wine, and who removes the leaven in our lives, we are no longer slaves. We are no longer bound to the mistakes of our pasts, our idols, our addictions, or our afflictions. There is a new creation transformation available to us. Now, *that* is good news.

The cleansing of the Temple is about the miracle of purification and freedom in your life. The secret is Yeshua as the unique Son of God, the "greater than Moses," being about His Father's business to cleanse His Father's House. Passover symbolizes Yeshua wanting to cleanse your life. He is saying, "Listen, I am the greater Temple. There's leaven in the Temple in Jerusalem, but there's no leaven in Me. And that's why when you destroy this Temple, and it's raised again, it is once and for all, for the fullness of redemption, healing, transformation, wholeness." It's time to come out and experience the fullness of freedom and purity in Him. A washing away of the past. A new you. And that's a beautiful thing.

# THREE

# THE SIGNS AND SECRETS
# OF NEW BIRTH

There's something miraculously wonderful about the birth of a baby. From conception, the seed grows inside the womb until we finally get to hold that new life in our hands. At what point does it become a living soul? After the birth of Cain, Eve said, "I have gotten a man with the help of the LORD" (Gen. 4:1 ESV). She recognized that something holy and miraculous had occurred and that God's hand was involved. Likewise, there is a spiritual birthing process for the things of God. A sculptor can sculpt a statue and make it amazingly lifelike, but it is still just a rock. Only God can breathe life into something lifeless.

The first chapter of Acts describes the days just after Yeshua rose from the dead. Acts 1:3 says, "To them [His disciples] He [Yeshua] showed Himself to be alive after His suffering through many convincing proofs, appearing to them for forty days and speaking about the kingdom of God." For forty days, Yeshua taught the disciples the mysteries and the meaning of the Kingdom. Why forty? Because the number 40 is related to full-term pregnancies, which last forty weeks. The first part of Acts is a season of birthing. God birthed something in the disciples, and I believe God wants to birth something new in you and through you. *Now* is a time of birthing.

But let's go back to the book of John, where we've seen Jesus turn water into wine and then cleanse the Temple. The next sign and mystery we'll explore is that of new birth, as Jesus described to Nicodemus. "Now there was a man," wrote John, "a Pharisee named Nicodemus, a ruler of the Jewish people. He came to *Yeshua* at night and said, 'Rabbi, we know that You, a teacher, have come from God. For no one can perform these signs which You do unless God is with Him!' *Yeshua* answered him, 'Amen, amen I tell you, unless one is born from above, he cannot see the kingdom of God'" (John 3:1–3).

Yeshua came to bring new life, though not yet a fully realized Kingdom. As Yeshua explained new life, Nicodemus wondered how a person could literally *rebirth* themselves.

## The Pharisees

To fully grasp the context of this miracle—this supernatural phenomenon known as being born anew or born again ("born from above" in the Tree of Life Version)—we need to understand the Pharisees, because Nicodemus was a Pharisee. Pharisees often play the part of the villain in Bible stories. However, Pharisees were trained Jewish holy men, and Yeshua's views would have closely aligned with the views of the Pharisees. The Pharisees were one of several predominant religious movements in the first century. They were centered in Jerusalem and were a Jewish renewal, or revival, movement. They wanted to see people walk closely in covenantal faith-fulness and deep understanding of the Scriptures and engage in prayer and spiritual life. Their vision and identity were rooted in God's call for His chosen people to be a royal priesthood and a holy nation. The Hebrew priests, also known as the *kohanim*, were required to live in a state of ritual purity to be able to minister in the Temple. However, the Pharisees believed that *all* Jews should live in a state of holiness and ritual purity because they were a priestly people.

## Extrabiblical Laws

Highly devout, the Pharisees were extremely zealous in their study and observance of the Torah—the five books of Moses. Their zeal for holiness and purity led them to what is known as "fencing the Torah." They created extrabiblical laws around the biblical commandments because they wanted to ensure that there was no way that the commandments of God could be broken. The kosher laws, *kashrut*, include "You are not to boil a young goat in its mother's milk" (Deut. 14:21; Ex. 23:19; 34:26). In pagan times, people would take a kid (young goat) and boil it in its mother's milk. This practice was prohibited for the people of Israel because it was connected to pagan rituals and seen as a form of cruelty. But the Pharisees "fenced the Torah" by changing this law to say the people couldn't mix milk and meat. Consequently, religious Jews do not eat cheeseburgers. The nonbib-lical commandments and legal rulings were based primarily on what is known as the traditions of the fathers. The goal of the Pharisaic law, known as *halakha*—how a person walks in the commandments found in the Torah—was to help every Israelite avoid sin and live a holy life as the priests were called to live. Those outside the party of the Pharisees were considered by the Pharisees as *am haaretz*, or "people of the land," which was an insult that described someone as ignorant, boorish, uneducated, or backward. Because of this, the typical Pharisee looked down on ignorant Jews.

## Repentance

The Pharisees believed that the Temple and the offering of the sacrifices in the Temple were foundational to the Torah. Still, they did not see those offerings as the most critical component to achieving atonement. They placed greater emphasis on *teshuvah*, repentance. To the Pharisees, true repentance was more important than the rituals of the Temple. That's why when the second Temple was destroyed in AD 70, a rabbi named Johanan ben Zakkai restructured Judaism to function without sacrifice because the Jews could only have sacrificed in the Temple. He said they were now offering prayers and repentance as the bulls ("offerings") of their lips, based on Hosea 14:3. The prophet Isaiah criticized Israel for offering sacrifices and confessions but not their hearts. He wrote, "So ADONAI says, 'Since these people draw near with their mouths and honor Me with their lips, yet their hearts are far from Me'" (Isa. 29:13). They were sacrificing and saying the right things, but their hearts were far from God. And so, a sacrifice without *teshuvah*, repentance, was of little value. But, as we'll see, there is a sacrifice needed for forgiveness. And Yeshua is ultimately that sacrifice.

## Perushim and Sadducees

In Hebrew, the word for Pharisee is *perushim* and means "the set-apart ones" or "separated ones." According to the Jewish historian Josephus, there were approximately six thousand members of the Pharisaic party.[1] They enjoyed widespread popularity and influence among the common religious Jewish people, leading the synagogues and educating the children.

The Sadducees, however, were considered the religious elite, the upper crust of society. Their members were from wealthy priestly families and had lost connection and interaction with the average Jew because they were stationed primarily inside the Temple. *The Lexham Bible Dictionary* tells us, "The Scriptures possessed supreme authority for the Sadducees, to the exclusion of oral traditions from former generations. The Sadducees denied the resurrection and the existence of fate."[2] They colluded with the Roman officials and were the go-betweens among the Jews and the Romans. The Sadducees were generally more influenced by Greco-Roman beliefs, thoughts, and customs than the Pharisees.

It's important to understand these groups as we study the context of Yeshua's frequent encounters with them.

## Yeshua and the Pharisees

In a sense, Yeshua was a Pharisee. Although He probably wasn't a formal member of the Pharisaic party, His beliefs and values were more closely aligned with those of the Pharisees than with any other Jewish religious sect. This is the reason there was so much conflict between the Pharisees and Yeshua. It is also why several prominent Pharisees attached themselves to Him and His teaching. We see this in John 3 with Nicodemus. We also see it with Joseph of Arimathea (John 19) and even with the apostle Paul, also known as Rabbi Sha'ul.

Understanding the beliefs and practices of the Pharisees is key to unlocking why Yeshua connected with them and why they were more open to the message of the Gospel than the priests. It helps us understand why Nicodemus was so interested in what Yeshua had to say. In contrast, we don't read about any priests or Sadducees coming to Yeshua and asking Him the types of questions Nicodemus asked. The priests were the main opposition to the Gospel both in the days of Yeshua and after His death, even for the first couple of centuries.

## Beliefs and Practices

To put this relationship in context, let's look at some of the beliefs and practices of the *perushim*, the Pharisees.

They worshiped and prayed three times daily: morning, noon, and night. This connected them to the three services in the Temple. They believed in free will and predestination, whereas the Sadducees believed in total free will. The Essenes, another, more mystical sect that resembled the Pharisees in many respects, believed in absolute predestination—that every act was predestined, or everyone who was going to be saved was to be predestined. But the Pharisees were more nuanced. They saw the truth of both free will and predestination and tried to balance the two. They believed that man has free will, but God has foreknowledge, and they wrestled with the tension between man's free will and the sovereignty of God.

The Pharisees believed in the supernatural, the existence of angels, the resurrection of the dead, and the afterlife. This is why Nicodemus was interested in discussing the Kingdom and spiritual birth with Yeshua. The Sadducees didn't believe that the soul lives on after death. They were rationalists heavily influenced by the Greek philosophy of that time, and they would not have been interested in Jesus' teaching.

There were different schools, or houses, of Pharisees. The two most famous were Beit Hillel and Beit Shammai. Hillel was more tolerant and lenient, while Shammai was stricter. These two houses formed the background for some of the debates we read about in the New Testament, such as the debate about divorce, when the Pharisees tried to trap Yeshua to find out whether He was liberal or legalistic (Matt. 19:3–12).

Studying Scripture was their highest form of worship, and it should also be for us. The word *disciple* means "student" in Greek and Hebrew. How can someone say they follow God or are godly if they're ignorant of who God is and what He requires? One of the great benefits I received from my Jewish heritage was respect for and knowledge of the Scriptures, which grew into love. This foundation played a critical role in my coming to see and accept Yeshua as the Messiah. We can't love someone if we don't know them. We can't be faithful and obedient to God if we don't know what He desires. This is why studying Scripture is so important. We also study the Word of God to renew our minds and to know God's mind and will.

Debating played a central role for the Pharisees, like the rabbis after them. The *Mishnah*, the early Jewish writings, includes the concept of "argument for the sake of heaven,"[3] which is an argument for the Kingdom's sake. This tells us that when these rabbis debated, it wasn't personal. Offense wasn't taken when two people disagreed; debates or disagreements were viewed as a form of iron sharpening iron. Sparks fly when iron sharpens iron—and that's a good thing! The Pharisees knew how to disagree. My experience, however, is that believers don't disagree well. We take disagreement personally; we become offended. We need to do better.

Nicodemus was asking questions to generate a dialogue with Yeshua. I would guess that in his mind, he was arguing for the sake of heaven. Let's find out more about him and his beliefs.

# Nicodemus

Because the Pharisees, not the Sadducees, believed in the supernatural—the afterlife, miracles, signs, and wonders—some wanted to understand who Jesus was and more about His teaching. When Paul was on trial in Jerusalem before the Sanhedrin, the religious council, he said, "I am a Pharisee, a son of Pharisees! I am on trial because of the hope of the resurrection of the dead!" (Acts 23:6). His words created a great uproar between the Pharisees and the Sadducees. Paul was brilliant in the way he handled that—because all Pharisees hope for the resurrection of the dead. It hit home.

Because Nicodemus was a Pharisee like Paul, we can better understand his mindset and why he was interested in Yeshua and His teaching. The Bible doesn't say much about him, but he comes across as a caring, sincere seeker of truth. There are only a handful of references to him in the New Testament. John 3:1 tells us Nicodemus was "a ruler of the Jewish people." But we find an interesting connection in Jewish tradition and history. There is a record of a man named Nicodemus ben Gurion. This is significant because Nicodemus is an unusual name. It wasn't common like David, Moses, or Miriam. And Nicodemus ben Gurion is mentioned in several Jewish sources. These sources describe him as a wealthy Jew who lived in Jerusalem during the first century—when Yeshua lived. He was one of the three wealthiest men in Jerusalem.[4]

If Nicodemus's name is Greek, we see that *Nico* comes from the word *nike*, which means "to have victory." Nike was the Greek goddess of victory. The word can also mean "to conquer." The Greek word *demus* means "people." So possible translations of Nicodemus's name are "victor of the people," "conqueror of the people," and "victory over the people." However, it's more probable that Nicodemus's name comes from the Hebrew, *Nakdimon ben Gurion*. The rabbis say this wasn't his real name, but he was given the name *Nakdimon* because this word signifies a breakthrough. He was given the name "breakthrough" on account of a miracle that happened in response to a prayer saying, "Make a miracle for me at the end of the day as You did at the beginning. Immediately, the wind blew and the clouds parted, and the sun was shining."[5]

We see that he was a Pharisee who was a member of the Sanhedrin, which is a religious ruling body of ancient Israel—it was the Supreme Court, the ultimate authority. Nicodemus wielded a lot of power and influence. Now we can more clearly grasp some of the context of John 3:

> Now there was a man, a Pharisee named Nicodemus, a ruler of the
> Jewish people. He came to Yeshua at night and said, "Rabbi, we know
> that You, a teacher, have come from God. For no one can perform these
> signs which You do unless God is with Him!" (vv. 1–2)

This was a man whose name meant *victory* and *breakthrough* and who was connected to something supernatural and miraculous. He held position as a wealthy Sanhedrin Pharisee. He was a man who had seen signs and miracles, yet he came to Yeshua at night. Why? Because he had a lot to lose. Many of the Pharisaic leaders were antagonistic toward Yeshua because people were flocking to Him, and He spoke and taught as One who had authority (Matt. 7:29). People were drawn to Yeshua's authority more than they were drawn to the Pharisees' authority. I'm sure there was some jealousy too. *Why flock to Him and not us? We're trained and educated and religious*, they may have thought. To be clear, this was an intra-family debate. This wasn't Yeshua being anti-Pharisee or anti-Jewish. Christians have had that mistaken view for too long, and the Pharisees have unfairly received a bad rap. When you read the book of Acts, it's the leading Pharisee of the day, Gamaliel, the teacher of Paul, who defended Peter and other disciples of Yeshua before the Sanhedrin. Gamaliel said, "Stay away from these men and leave them alone. For if this plan or undertaking is of men, it will come to an end; but if it is of God, you will not be able to stop them. You might even be found fighting against God" (Acts 5:38–39).

The first believers faced real hostility from the priests, yet there were religious leaders like Gamaliel, who likely heard Yeshua's teachings, saw His miracles, and wanted to know more. Most likely, Nicodemus represented a group of Pharisees when he approached Yeshua at night. They had questions, but it was risky to talk with Yeshua. It wasn't good for one's reputation to be caught with Him. On top of that, it was dangerous. After all, Yeshua had cleansed the Temple and challenged the ruling authorities, calling them corrupt. These men ultimately crucified Yeshua. They weren't playing games. They were out for blood, and I'm sure all this was running through Nicodemus's mind.

The ruling priests were gunning for Yeshua, and perhaps Nicodemus drew the short straw to be the one to meet with Him. That's why Nicodemus approached Him at night. I've known a few Jewish people who only wanted to meet with me in private to discuss Yeshua, to keep the matter secret. One was an assistant of a great Hasidic rabbi from one of the leading Hasidic dynasties, who came to know Yeshua, but he would only meet secretly out of fear of exposure. He didn't want to risk becoming an outcast and everything that would come along with that for him and his family. Surely we can understand why Nicodemus did what he did.

## Traveling from Darkness to Light

Yes, Nicodemus had a lot to lose. That's why he came to Yeshua under the cloak of darkness. But there's something more to consider than just his secrecy. There's a spiritual symbolism in this idea of night. In one sense, Nicodemus was in the dark because he didn't have the full revelation of who Yeshua was. As we read in a later chapter, after the resurrection, the disciples were fishing at night and caught nothing (John 21). They couldn't wrap their minds around the events that had just happened, so they were fishing in the dark, just as Nicodemus was spiritually in the dark.

In Jewish thought, night represents exile, and light represents redemption. During the years of exile, the people of Israel were symbolically living in the dark. Even Yeshua referred to the idea of being in the night of exile and everything that comes with it. The three hours of darkness on the cross is in part Yeshua taking spiritual exile on Himself to redeem us from exile and darkness. Yeshua is the greater than Moses, Passover Lamb, and God's firstborn Son who died to redeem and rescue us from the exile of our personal Egypt. Hell is both the ultimate form as well as the ultimate result of exile and is connected to darkness (Matt. 22:13).[6] We see this connection between night and Creation. In Genesis 1, we see "there was evening and there was morning—one day" (v. 5). Amid the darkness, God said, "Let there be light!" (v. 3). Just as Creation happened out of darkness, so people become new creations out of the darkness. The new creation has experienced salvation and is moving from the kingdom of darkness to the kingdom of light. Nicodemus was on a journey from darkness to light. He was moving from the place of formlessness and void and chaos. And God was about to say, "Let there be light!" The light bulb was going on within Nicodemus, and the night was about to give way to Yeshua's miracle of light and new birth.

All of us experience times of darkness. Before we come to know the Lord, we're living in darkness. I remember when the light clicked on for me that Yeshua was my Savior, the Messiah. Even though I had been raised in the Jewish tradition, there was a veil over my eyes until illumination came. Yeshua said, "The people sitting in darkness have seen a great light, and those sitting in the region and shadow of death, on them a light has dawned" (Matt. 4:16). When we come to Yeshua, we come into the light; we come out of the night. But coming out of the night is a lifelong process of understanding who He is.

## Acknowledging the Rabbi as Messiah

Nicodemus said, "Rabbi, we know that You, a teacher, have come from God" (John 3:2). Here, he showed respect to Yeshua by calling Him Rabbi—Teacher. Nicodemus and the group he likely represented understood that Yeshua was a teacher sent by God because He taught with great authority and wisdom far above the other rabbis. When Yeshua opened His mouth, people tuned in as they felt the weight of God's Word and the Lord's presence. When He cleansed the Temple, He had the boldness (*chutzpah*) and great authority to remove the leaven. Either He was crazy (*meshugenah*), or He was the Messiah sent by God to act and speak with this type of authority. Nicodemus said to Him, "No one can perform these signs which You do unless God is with Him!" (John 3:2). Yeshua's miraculous signs made it clear that He was not crazy but was sent from heaven.

It's one thing to say you're *going to do* miracles. It's quite another to *do* them for everyone to see. When I was studying in my messianic Jewish studies program for a season in Chicago, a guy came to our school wearing a *kippah* (head covering) and a *tallit* (prayer shawl), saying he was the Messiah. Amused, I responded, "Really? So how are you going to prove you're the Messiah?" He said, "Palm trees are going to grow in Chicago in the middle of winter." Of course, palm trees never grew. It's cold in Chicago! The man was just crazy. Yeshua, however, wasn't *meshugenah*.

He performed the miracles. He loved to show and tell, to demonstrate the Kingdom of God and His power, like turning the water into wine.

## The Heart of Nicodemus's Question

Nicodemus was just about to ask Yeshua a question when Yeshua answered it—something we see Him doing throughout the Gospels. Yeshua knows the hearts of people. He understands them even before they say anything. Yeshua knows the questions in people's hearts, so we don't need to be afraid to ask God our questions. His knowing is part of the miracle that was happening in John 3. Yeshua's getting to the heart of Nicodemus's question before he even voiced it further demonstrated that God had sent Him. Who wouldn't want to listen to someone who could look in their eyes and answer every question in their heart—even the unspoken and challenging ones? That's what I love about Yeshua. He doesn't shy away from the hard questions. The whole Bible is about dealing with hard things. Who can forget Job, who threw his questions up to God concerning the pain he was experiencing? God not only answered Job but threw questions back at Job, causing him to think deeper. In the end, though, God didn't punish Job for asking hard questions; He vindicated him.[7] Yeshua is okay with us bringing Him our honest questions. He already knows what's in our hearts anyway. So when Nicodemus acknowledged that Jesus is from God, Jesus went straight to what was on his heart.

### Born from Above: Rebirth

Yeshua replied, "Amen, amen I tell you, unless one is born from above, he cannot see the kingdom of God" (John 3:3). Here, we see the concept of being born again. But Nicodemus wanted to know the answers to the questions that all of us have asked for some time: *How do I know I'm right with God? How do I know God cares for me? How do I know where I stand with God? How can I know with certainty that I have eternal life?* Nicodemus didn't understand Yeshua's answer. He probably thought Yeshua was testing him. So he responded, "How can a man be born when he is old? . . . He cannot enter his mother's womb a second time and be born, can he?" (v. 4).

Yeshua continued, "You're a teacher of Israel and you do not understand these things?" (v. 10). Although Yeshua certainly brought something new and powerful to the concept of being born again, it wasn't completely foreign to the rabbis. A Gentile who converts to Judaism is considered as a newborn child. In a sense, he is born anew into the Jewish faith. Some Jews think it was an actual supernatural birth; others think it was not an actual birth but a change in status. This must have seemed insulting to Nicodemus, a learned student of the Torah. He knew that Gentiles, pagans who were not raised as members of the covenant, had to be born like a child into the Jewish faith. He couldn't understand why Yeshua would say that he—a Jew born into the covenant—would also need to be reborn.

"Amen, amen I tell you," Yeshua said, "unless one is born of water and spirit, he cannot enter the kingdom of God" (v. 5). The phrase "Amen, amen" is significant. In Hebrew, the word *amen* is derived from the same word as *faith* (*emunah* means faith and the root Hebrew word is *eman*, meaning "to confirm"). In fact, Jewish people think *amen* is an acronym for *El melekh ne'eman*: "God is a faithful King." Using the word *amen* is like saying, "Everything I'm saying is true."

Nicodemus (remember, the name is a combination of the Greek *nike*, meaning "victory," and *demos*, meaning "common people") directly connected to the pilgrims who traveled to Jerusalem to celebrate the holidays. As I mentioned earlier, Nicodemus experienced a miracle involving water and causing the sun to reappear after it had set. The Feast of Sukkot, where the miracle happened, is where he got his name. Yeshua then said, "What is born of the flesh is flesh, and what is born of the Spirit is spirit. Do not be surprised that I said to you, 'You all must be born from above'" (vv. 6–7). Nicodemus was clearly confused. Let's try to understand why.

## The Birth of Israel

We can learn about rebirth from Israel's history. They went into Egypt with seventy individuals, Exodus 1 tells us: "Now these are the names of *Bnei-Yisrael* who came into Egypt with Jacob, each man with his family. . . . The souls that came out of the line of Jacob numbered 70 in all, while Joseph was already in Egypt" (vv. 1, 5). Consider that Israel went in as a group of only seventy souls but came out numbering in the millions!

The word for Egypt in Hebrew is *Mitzraim,* "a place of confinement or restriction." *Mitzraim* comes from the root word *tzur,* which means "rock." In Jewish thought, Egypt is considered the womb of civilization. The people of Israel were in exile for about four hundred years. Four hundred is a multiple of forty. And forty weeks is a full-term pregnancy. So, they were in Egypt symbolically as a full-term pregnancy—not weeks but years. Egypt was the womb. The ten plagues brought on the Egyptians were the labor pains, the shaking and quaking. When the Israelites left Egypt, they went in great haste. (This is one of the reasons we eat *matzah,* unleavened bread—they left so quickly that their bread did not have time to rise.) They were instructed to eat the Passover with their loins girded and their staffs in hand.

Pregnancy can seem to be taking forever for expectant parents, and then *boom!* The baby comes—often with little warning, in the middle of the night or while we're fully engaged in something else. We can use the human birth process as an analogy for the birth of Israel. The parting of the Red Sea was like the woman's water breaking. Israel going through the Red Sea was like the baby going through the birth canal. The water closing on the Egyptian army after Israel had passed through is symbolic of God washing away their past. The old was passing away, and the new was coming. The water closed, and they could not go back to Egypt. He was birthing them from an enslaved people into a redeemed and free nation.

As Israel could not physically return to Egypt, neither can we physically return into our mothers' wombs. The people of Israel were born naturally with some divine intervention. To grow as a nation—the people of Abraham, Isaac, and Jacob—the twelve tribes had to have a physical birth. But they were not born supernaturally as a free nation until they escaped Egypt. And so they had two births. They were naturally birthed through Abraham, Isaac, and Jacob, and they went to Egypt. God used their time in Egypt to birth them as a redeemed nation and caused a supernatural multiplication—incredibly, from seventy to millions. This is what we read in Exodus 1:6–7:

> Then Joseph died, as did all his brothers and all that generation. Yet *Bnei-Yisrael* were fruitful, increased abundantly, multiplied and grew extremely numerous—so the land was filled with them.

The more the Egyptians afflicted and oppressed the people of Israel, the more they multiplied. The word in Hebrew translated "multiplied" (*rabah*) means "broke through" or "burst forth." They had to endure affliction and oppression to experience a breakthrough—a new birth.

As Israel was twice-birthed, so we and Nicodemus need to have two births—a natural, physical birth and a supernatural, spiritual one.

## Breakthrough

Being born anew is the key to a breakthrough. It's the key to overcoming. God wants to do this new spiritual work in you. Some people might claim to be born again. The question is, Are you walking in the spiritual power and authority of what that means? God wants to renew you so that He can do something new in you. It is possible to be born again and still maintain a slave mindset. Therefore, the apostle Paul urged us "to put off your old self . . . to be made new in the attitude of your minds; and to put on the new self, created to be like God in true righteousness and holiness" (Eph. 4:22–24 NIV). You can choose to put on the God mindset and walk in the freedom He has for you.

Even if you are beat down and oppressed, God's promise can still multiply you and cause you to spread out and increase. Even persecution can't stop the promise of multiplication and increase. If you're in labor pains, if you're in the process of God birthing something new in you, if you're being oppressed or mistreated, don't worry! God can multiply you and use your affliction to bring about His promises and birth something in you.

Just as Israel needed a new birth to grow from a family to a nation, from slaves to sons and daughters of God, every one of us as individuals needs to be born again. There is a physical birth, which represents earth. And there is a spiritual birth, which represents heaven.

This concept goes back to Creation. God created the heavens and the earth, both a spiritual and a physical reality. There is a body, and the body is a container for the soul. What we do with the physical body and the soul within it in this life helps us experience life in this world and eternal life with Him forever. When we are born again, it's a miracle. It is a coming together of heaven and earth to produce life and blessing like in the beginning before the Fall. When you are born anew, God takes residency in you. You have the "Messiah in you, the hope of glory!" (Col. 1:27). As we reflect on this, and the good news Yeshua gave to Nicodemus, we see that this new birth is truly a miracle.

# FOUR

# THE SIGNS AND SECRETS
# OF THE SERPENT

Nicodemus the Pharisee came to Yeshua in the night, seeking clear answers. Instead, Yeshua revealed to him mysteries and miracles, without Nicodemus even asking. Every part of this conversation has significance. We've already explored the unfathomable miracle of new birth that was revealed to Nicodemus in John 3: "Unless one is born from above, he cannot see the kingdom of God" (v. 3). Nicodemus asked, "How can these things happen?" (v. 9). By way of an answer, Yeshua started to explain: "No one has gone up into heaven except the One who came down from heaven—the Son of Man. Just as Moses lifted up the serpent in the desert," said Yeshua, "so the Son of Man must be lifted up" (vv. 13–14). Why on earth would Yeshua compare Himself to the serpent on the pole? We need to know because this is a foundational scriptural truth that often doesn't get enough attention. What does it mean, and what's the deeper spiritual significance? In the sign and secret of the serpent, we find a remarkably well-designed connection between the Old Testament and New, between Moses and the Messiah, that reveals new depths in what Yeshua has done for us and the miraculous power He has today to atone, to provide, to heal, and to transform. As we explore the image of the serpent, we find that God has much to reveal to us.

## What Is the Serpent on the Pole?

In His conversation with Nicodemus, Yeshua built on the idea that He was the greater Moses—the true Messiah: "Just as Moses lifted up the serpent in the desert, so the Son of Man must be lifted up, so that whoever believes in Him may have eternal life!" (John 3:14–15). What is the meaning of this mystery of the serpent on the pole? On the surface, it seems like a strange analogy that Yeshua made. But all of this is based on Numbers 21:4–9, the account of the Children of Israel wandering through the desert. And clearly, they were becoming disgruntled.

They travelled from Mount Hor along the route to the Sea of Reeds in order to go around the land of Edom. The spirit of the people became impatient along the way.

The people spoke against God and Moses: "Why have you brought us from Egypt to die in the wilderness, because there is no bread, no water, and our very spirits detest the despicable food [manna]?" So ADONAI sent poisonous serpents among the people, and they bit the people and many of the people of Israel died.

The people came to Moses and said, "We sinned when we spoke against ADONAI and you! Pray to ADONAI for us, that He may take away the snakes!" So Moses prayed for the people.

ADONAI said to Moses, "Make yourself a fiery snake and put it on a pole. Whenever anyone who has been bitten will look at it, he will live."

So Moses made a bronze snake and put it on a pole, and it happened that whenever a snake bit anyone and he looked at the bronze snake, he lived.

A harrowing story. Why would God do this? And why would God instruct Moses to make a bronze serpent and put it on a pole to represent salvation? More to the point, why did Yeshua connect Himself to this act of Moses? The first thing to understand is that Yeshua said, "As Moses lifted up the serpent." The Hebrew word for "to lift up" is *nasa*. It can mean "to lift up," but it can also mean "to bear," "to carry," or "to forgive." The meaning in John 3:14 is "to bear" or "to carry" sin and guilt. In the Jewish system of atonement, a scapegoat was offered in the Temple, on the Day of Atonement, to make atonement for the people; the goat carried the sins of the people: "The goat will carry [*nasa*] all their iniquities by itself into a solitary land and he is to leave the goat in the wilderness" (Lev. 16:22). The Hebrew word *nasa* is one of the most critical words connected to salvation.

As a side note, we could say the English abbreviation NASA, the National Aeronautics and Space Administration, gives us the mental picture of lifting off, taking off, or going higher into outer space. That's what the cross does for us. It causes us to blast off, to be able to leave earth, to go from death to life, from darkness into light, to go into the heavens where we've never gone before. Yeshua was lifted up on the cross because He bore our sin like the scapegoat, just like the serpent on the pole.

## The Messiah on the Cross

Isaiah 53:4 says, "Surely He has borne our griefs and carried our pains. Yet we esteemed Him stricken, struck by God, and afflicted." When it says He "carried our pains," the word for carried is *nasa*. In the Hebrew New Testament, the serpent in the wilderness was "lifted up" (*nasa*), and it bore the sins of the people who were grumbling. And as they lifted up (*nasa*) their eyes to look at that serpent, they found healing. When the Messiah was lifted up (*nasa*) on the cross, as the serpent was lifted up on the pole, He bore our sin and our pain, and it was for our gain. Just like the people who looked at the serpent on the pole found healing, when we look to Yeshua on the cross, we find healing and wholeness. So, Isaiah 53—one of the most important messianic prophecies—connects back to the serpent on the pole in the wilderness. The serpent on the pole connects back to the scapegoat, which in turn connects to the cross, where the Messiah would bear our griefs and carry our pains.

Why would Yeshua need to be lifted up like the serpent on the pole, as He revealed to Nicodemus? Think about it. The first man and woman stole from the tree in the Garden of Eden. When Adam and Eve took fruit down from the tree, it was a descent. There was a lowering spiritually, morally, physically, emotionally, and relationally—on every level. When humankind pulled that fruit off the tree and disobeyed God's command, they dragged themselves and all of creation, including us, down. So the Messiah had to descend from heaven, and He had to be lifted back up onto the tree for you and me. When He was lifted up, He was placed back on that tree to replace what we stole from the tree; He was placed on the cross to atone for the sin of the first man and woman and to redeem and repair us. I don't know about you, but I think what He did for us on that cross was amazing—a miracle. It brings to mind the words of Moses and the Israelites, singing to the Lord: *Mi kamocha ba'elim Adonai, Mi kamocha nedar ba'qodesh, Nora tehillot oseh fele.* Or, "Who is like You among the gods, Lord? Who is like You, majestic in holiness, Awesome in praises, working wonders?" (Ex. 15:11 NASB). We brought a descent, and Yeshua descended so that we could ascend. But of course, there's more.

## The Revealed and Concealed Torah

Nicodemus came to Yeshua, who was a rabbi, a teacher of the Torah. There are two aspects of the Torah: the *revealed* Torah (*nigleh*) and the hidden, or *concealed*, Torah (*nistar*). In other words, that which we can know and that which is mystical. Rabbis studied the revealed and concealed aspects of the Torah and the Scriptures. We base this idea on Deuteronomy 29:28: "The secret things belong to ADONAI our God, but the things revealed belong to us and to our children forever—in order to do all the words of this *Torah*." In His explanation to Nicodemus about being born again, Yeshua essentially said, "Nicodemus, if you can't even comprehend the revealed things, how will you understand the deeper revelation of the concealed things?" (John 3:10–12, author's paraphrase).

Proverbs 25:2 says, "It is the glory of God to conceal a matter and the glory of kings to search it out." As Children of the King, we can't just settle for the simple truths of Scripture. It is our glory to search out the concealed things, the deeper meanings, the deeper truths about Yeshua and the things He taught. That is the fusion of the old and the new coming together. When we search for deeper truths, we are not settling for half an inheritance. God conceals some things so that we would seek them—so that He would ultimately reveal them to us, so we would find Him. Hebrews 11:6 says, "But without faith it is impossible to please Him, for he who comes to God must believe that He is, and that He is a rewarder of those who diligently seek Him" (NKJV). God rewards those who diligently seek Him. What is the reward? It could be several things. Illumination, understanding, more truth, but first and foremost, the reward is Himself. God wants to reveal the wonders of Himself to us, but He wants to be sought. There's a concealing and a revealing, and concealing is for the sake of revealing!

## The Secret of Ascending and Descending

What are the deeper things that were once concealed but Yeshua was revealing? In John 3:13 He said to Nicodemus, "No one has gone up into heaven except the One who came down from heaven—the Son of Man." Being born again, which is the result of salvation, can come only through the One who ascended to and descended from heaven.

In Jewish thought, *ascending* and *descending* are associated with Moses. An ancient Aramaic translation of the Bible known as the Targum helps us understand this association.[1] Aramaic was one of the primary languages of the Jewish people from the time they went into Babylonian captivity, because Aramaic was the primary language of the Babylonians. When Ezra and Nehemiah returned to Jerusalem, most of the people couldn't speak Hebrew; they could only speak Aramaic. The Aramaic translation of the Bible helps us understand the thinking and the writings of the New Testament authors. We can look to the Targum to help us understand what Yeshua was talking about when He mentioned ascending and descending, things that are revealed and concealed. An English translation of the *Targum Jerusalem* says this:

> The law [Torah] is not in the heavens, that thou shouldst say, O that we had one like Mosheh [Moses] the prophet to ascend into heaven, and bring it (down) to us, and make us hear its commands, that we may do

them! Neither is the law beyond the great sea, that thou shouldst say, O that we had one like Jonah the prophet, who could descend into the depths of the sea, and bring it to us, and make us hear its commands, that we may do them! For the word is very nigh you, in your mouth, that you may meditate upon it, and in your hearts, that you may perform it. (Deuteronomy 30.12–14)[2]

In Hebraic and rabbinic thought, the ascending and descending associated with both Moses (who ascended and descended from Mount Sinai) and Jonah (who descended into the seas in the whale) connect to the Messiah because the Messiah was, again, prophesied to be greater than Moses. The Jewish leaders and people were looking for the One who would ascend and descend like Moses; they were looking for the prophet who would descend, the greater than Jonah. Yeshua Himself said to a group of Torah scholars and Pharisees, "An evil and adulterous generation clamors for a sign, yet no sign shall be given to it except the sign of Jonah the prophet. For just as Jonah was in the belly of the great fish for three days and three nights, so the Son of Man will be in the heart of the earth for three days and three nights" (Matt. 12:39–40). Yeshua was connecting Himself to the prophecies of the Messiah.

Yeshua used the imagery of ascending (*aliyah*) and descending (*yeridah*) to connect Himself to Moses, Jonah, and the Messiah.[3] The word for ascending (*aliyah*) is used to describe "going up" to Jerusalem. The *Targum Jerusalem* says this:

And His Word will accept your repentance with favor, and will have mercy upon you, and He will gather you again from all the nations whither the Lord your God has scattered you. Though you may be dispersed unto the ends of the heavens, from thence will the Word of the Lord gather you together by the hand of Elijah the great priest, and from thence will He bring you by the hand of the King Meshiha [Messiah]. (Deuteronomy 30.3–4)[4]

John wrote, "In the beginning was the Word. The Word was with God, and the Word was God" (John 1:1). John was writing about the Messiah, the Word. The Aramaic translation uses "the Word" as one of the names of God. It's not using "the Word of the Lord" to refer to the Bible; it's calling the Messiah the Word of the Lord or God. God was going to cause Israel to ascend—to make *aliyah*—by "His Word." This is incredible! Ascending and descending point to the Messiah as a greater than Moses who will ascend to bring the true understanding of the revealed and concealed aspects of the Torah. He'll bring both the messianic Torah and the plain Torah, meaning He'll bring out the deeper mysteries of the Scriptures and the work of redemption and salvation. The Messiah is the Word of the Lord!

Moses ascended and descended Mount Ṣinai, but Yeshua is even greater. He descended from and ascended into heaven. When He spoke to Nicodemus about the serpent being lifted up on the pole, Yeshua was not only saying that He was greater than Moses. He was saying He is God's divine Son, the divine Word that would fulfill the Jewish understanding that it was by the Word of the Lord and by the hand of King Messiah that these things would occur.

Yeshua's ascending and descending reveal His identity as God's divine Son. Proverbs 30:4 says, "Who has gone up into heaven, and come down? Who has gathered the wind in the palm of His hand? Who has wrapped the waters in a cloak? Who has established all the ends of the earth? What is His name and what is the name of His son—if you know?" The question "Who has gone up into heaven and come down?" is answered. The mysterious secret that had been hidden for centuries was being revealed. "The name of His son" was and is Yeshua.

## The Numeric Connection

There's an interesting numeric play on words going on here, as Jesus was speaking to Nicodemus in John 3. We know that Hebrew is alphanumeric. There's another reason why God told Moses to put a serpent on a pole and why Yeshua compared Himself to the serpent on the pole, and it reveals ever-deeper levels of God's intentionality.

### The Secret of the Holy and Evil Serpent

The Hebrew word for Messiah (*Mashiach*) has a numeric value of 358. The Hebrew word for serpent (*nachash*) also equals 358. As our sages taught, the Messiah is the archenemy of Satan. Why is this significant? The Messiah (358) is the cure for the curse that came through the serpent in the Garden of Eden (358). The evil serpent (358) is overcome and defeated by the Messiah (358), who is, symbolically, the holy serpent. We see a connection to Moses because when Moses first went to Pharaoh, Moses threw down his staff and it became a serpent. Then the Egyptian magicians threw down their staffs and they became serpents. But here's the difference: Moses' staff that became a serpent ate up the magicians' serpents (Ex. 4–7). Why is that significant? It's symbolic of life swallowing up death. The Messiah is the holy serpent who swallows up the evil serpent. The Messiah swallows up death and brings life. That's a part of the deeper mystery.

Like the Israelites who looked at the bronze serpent, which was a symbol of divine salvation, healing from heaven, one must look at the Messiah (358) to find salvation. The numeric value of the words *bronze serpent (nakhash nekhoshet)* is 1,116. This number corresponds to a famous list of names for Yeshua: the divine identity of Messiah as revealed in one of the key messianic prophecies, Isaiah 9:5: "For to us a child is born, a son will be given to us, and the government will be upon His shoulder. His Name will be called Wonderful Counselor, Mighty God, My Father of Eternity, Prince of Peace." The Hebrew phrase translated as "Wonderful Counselor, Mighty God, My Father of Eternity, Prince of Peace" equals 1,116. The bronze serpent equals 1,116, and the identity of the Messiah equals 1,116. The bronze serpent (1,116) points to the divine identity of the Messiah and the fulfillment of Isaiah 9:5. Coincidence? Again, all these numbers point to the preciseness of our God. Numbers and math are the universal language, and many apologists and philosophers argue mathematics exists independent of humans. The hidden coding of the universe is made up of numbers. Galileo wrote, "Mathematics is the language in which God has written the universe."[5] It makes sense, then, that God would use numbers as part of His language to reveal secrets about Himself in the Bible.

## The Royal Crown

When Yeshua compared Himself to the bronze serpent in the wilderness, He revealed that He's the Messiah who overcomes the serpent. I find it astonishing that the numeric value points back to "Wonderful Counselor, Mighty God, My Father of Eternity, Prince of Peace." In addition, the Hebrew for *royal crown (keter malkhut)* equals 1,116. So, 1,116 points to the King of Israel, the Messiah, who wears David's royal crown. Therefore, the bronze serpent points to the royal crown; it points to the

Messiah. By the means of His death and being lifted up like the serpent, the Messiah was to restore the crown to the Kingdom. Because He was lifted up, He deserves to wear the crown. This is what the apostle Paul wrote in Philippians 2:5–11.

Yeshua's descent was for the sake of His ascent. Other biblical figures went through this process too. Joseph had to descend into the pit to ascend to the palace. David had to be rejected by his family and King Saul. All that rejection and descending were for his ascending the throne. The same is true for the Messiah. And it is true of you and me: every descent you go through in life—every death or loss you experience—is for the sake of ascent. Your rejection is for the sake of your promotion.

When I came to California, it was to pursue and fulfill the vision God placed in my heart. Like Joseph sharing his dream with his brothers, I shared mine with many, even with some I deeply respected. Also like Joseph, I was rejected, ridiculed, and discouraged. I wondered if I had missed God. However, He was working to bring me to His place and plan, which was far better than I could imagine. So don't be discouraged by your descent, but understand that God has an ascent, a promotion, and wants to lift you up. May we say, with the psalmist, "I will exalt You, ADONAI, for You have lifted me up, and did not let my enemies gloat over me" (Ps. 30:2).

The One who wears the royal crown (1,116) indeed lifts us up. Not only that, but He re-creates us. There is even more to discover here.

The number 1,116 is the value of the first two Hebrew words of Genesis 1:1, *bereishit bara*, which translates as "in the beginning He created." As I mentioned in my book *Mysteries of the Messiah*, the words *bereshit bara* can be read not as "in the beginning" but "on account of the firstborn He [God the Father] created the world." This fact means that God only created the world because the Messiah agreed to die before He created the world. That's why the book of Revelation says the Messiah is the Lamb slain before the foundation of the world (13:8). God wasn't going to create the world unless the Messiah agreed to die, because God always makes sure the cure exists before the sickness comes. Before the sickness of the curse of the Fall came into the world, He already had the remedy: the Messiah's death, the serpent on the pole, the One who was going to be lifted up for us. *Bereshit bara* can also be read, "Through the firstborn son He created." The Hebrew can be read "through the firstborn Son God created the world." Being born again means we become a new creation. When we have faith like the Israelites who saw the serpent on the pole and believed and were healed, we are re-created through faith in the Messiah's death and resurrection. God wants to do a re-creation, a new creation, in you—*bereshit bara* (1,116), through the Wonderful Counselor, Mighty God, My Father of Eternity, Prince who wears the royal crown, who is like the bronze serpent.

## We Are Royalty Through Faith in Yeshua

If Yeshua indeed wears the royal crown, it means something life-changing for us. Yeshua said that we become children of the King when we place our faith in Him. If you're a child of the King, you are royalty; it is part of your birthright and that royal calling on your life to search these things out. According to Deuteronomy, Moses wrote that every king of Israel needed to write a Torah scroll (17:18). David embodied this aspect of royalty. He meditated on the Torah day and night. God revealed Himself supernaturally to David, used David in supernatural ways, and anointed David as king. As royalty, through our faith in the Messiah, we discover that there are deeper, significant mysteries and meanings that God wants to reveal to us. Another aspect of walking in that royalty is allowing God to use us in supernatural ways. When He reveals His mysteries and will, we can expect miracles to follow us!

## The Serpent Transformed

What can we take from this miracle of the serpent Jesus revealed to Nicodemus? First, the Messiah died for us and was lifted up on the cross, just as we are lifted up in Him. Second, Yeshua explained to Nicodemus, and us in turn, that He was indeed the Messiah, and greater than Moses. Third, He defeated the work of the evil serpent in the Garden of Eden. He swallowed up death that we may live. The evil serpent is overcome by the Messiah, who is the holy serpent. Remember, the serpent connects to Moses directly because Moses was the first redeemer whose staff turned into a serpent. Part of the miracle is that the dead, inanimate staff of Moses came to life, and God used it to swallow up the living serpents of the Egyptian magicians. Moses' serpent on the pole and Moses' staff that became a serpent point to the Messiah (358), who symbolizes the life that will swallow up death, which is represented by the Egyptian serpent (358). Isaiah 25:8 says, "He will swallow up death forever." And the apostle Paul wrote, "Death is swallowed up in victory" (1 Cor. 15:54).

Yeshua wants us to experience not just salvation but also transformation. From strength to strength and glory to glory, He wants to radically change our lives to become more like Him, bearing His image. And bearing His image and becoming like Him is one of the keys to walking in your royal identity and destiny as Children of the King. To be an image bearer of God means bearing the image of Yeshua. Bearing His image involves conforming to His likeness—thinking like He thinks, walking like He walked, living like Yeshua lived, acting as He acted. Because Scripture transforms our minds, the key is understanding both the revealed and concealed aspects of Scripture. We must dig deep into the Word to comprehend the mysterious and hidden things. We do this with the help of the Holy Spirit, whose power causes us to be born again and illuminates the Scriptures. The Holy Spirit opens our hearts to everything in the Word.

Being born again is a miracle of God, and Scripture is also a miracle—it had to be revealed by God. When God opens our eyes to His Word, and we start seeing connections between the Old and New Testaments, it's a miracle that shows us incredible truths that change and transform us. When God reveals Himself to us through His Word, it should cause our hearts to burn within us as it did for the disciples on the road to Emmaus. We start to recognize Him in the clues He has placed for us. That is one of the miracles in the symbol of the serpent. And it is one that shows the completeness of His work and the mysteries God uses to bring wonder to our hearts.

# FIVE

# THE SIGNS AND SECRETS

# OF HEALING

We've been discovering that the book of John is the book of signs. John even concluded with this fact: "*Yeshua* performed many other signs in the presence of the disciples, which are not written in this book. But these things have been written so that you may believe that *Yeshua* is *Mashiach Ben-Elohim* [Messiah, the Son of God], and that by believing you may have life in His name" (John 20:30–31). We've already covered a few of Yeshua's works in other chapters. Now we'll look at the healing at the pool of Bethesda, which is the third of Yeshua's signs or miracles in the book of John—one that brings our belief to new levels.

John 5:1–13 tells us Yeshua was in Jerusalem after celebrating Pentecost, or *Shavuot*, when He healed a needy man on the Sabbath (v. 9). The man was by a pool called Bethesda, or "house of mercy or grace" in the Hebrew/Aramaic. At that time many people believed the waters had the power to cure sickness and infirmity, but this man, after lying by the pool for thirty-eight years, could not take full advantage of those healing properties. Yeshua asked the invalid, "Do you want to get well?" (v. 6). The man gave an excuse but Yeshua told him to "pick up [his] mat and walk" (v. 8). The Jewish leaders were angry and could not understand why Yeshua would heal on the Sabbath. Let's dig a bit deeper into the story of this healing to better understand.

## The Significance of the Jewish Feast

Right before this miracle occurred, Yeshua had gone to Jerusalem to celebrate a *chag* (holiday). Scripture doesn't specify what *chag* He was celebrating, but knowing which Jewish feast was happening during this time is key to mining the depths of this miracle. In Jerusalem, there was a place by the pool called the sheep gate (Neh. 3:1, 32; 12:39). The name was symbolic because the blind, lame, and disabled individuals near this gate were not even as valuable as sheep. These individuals were considered like sheep without a shepherd. Nobody cared about them. But here came Yeshua, the Good Shepherd, who cared about these broken sheep who were societal outcasts.

There was a certain man at the pool who could not walk. Yeshua asked him, "Do you want to get well?" That seems like a crazy question. Of course! Who wouldn't want to get well? This guy had been unable to walk for thirty-eight years. Life expectancy in the first century was only about forty. He'd lived his entire life without the ability to walk and had lost hope. Hal Lindsey has been quoted as saying, "Man can live about forty days without food, about three days without water, about eight minutes without air, but only for one second without hope."[1] And what is hope? Hope is the belief that your future will be different and better than your past. This man was hopeless. He thought, *Nothing's going to change for me. It's been thirty-eight years. Besides, I probably won't be around much longer.* Just look at his response to Yeshua's question: "Sir, I have nobody to put me into the pool when the water is stirred up. While I'm trying to get in, somebody else steps down before me!" (v. 7). Notice that he didn't offer Yeshua an answer; he offered Him an excuse. He offered a justification. Yeshua didn't ask, "Why are you not well?" It seems like the man didn't understand what Yeshua was asking. He was asking, "Do you *want* to be made well?"

As many of us have realized, hope deferred makes the heart sick (Prov. 13:12). You may be single and waiting for that soulmate to appear for what seems like a lifetime. Or the dream you've longed for hasn't come to pass. Life hurts sometimes. We are broken. But when God fulfills a desire, it is like a tree of life blooming. Hope fulfilled leads to life. Yeshua is the ultimate hope dealer. He loves to give hope to the hopeless. That's what He was giving to the man at the pool of Bethesda. The man felt stuck and as if he had no future. In a sense, he was trapped, like Israel had been trapped and enslaved in Egypt. The good news is that there's hope—hope for him, for you, for your family, for your friends. It doesn't matter how long you've been "stuck" dealing with a particular pain or problem. There's always hope. Pentecost, like most Jewish holidays, is, in part, a celebration of hope. At Pentecost God gave the Children of Israel the Ten Commandments—hope from God's presence and His desire to build a foundation of the nation. Pentecost (Acts 2) also gave the disciples hope with the coming of the Holy Spirit.

## Pilgrimage Holidays

John 5:1 says, "After this there was a Jewish feast, and *Yeshua* went up to Jerusalem." The question is, What holiday was John referring to? There are three pilgrimage holidays: (1) *Pesach*, or Passover; (2) *Shavuot*, or Pentecost; and (3) *Sukkot*, the Feast of Tabernacles (Ex. 23:14). I don't believe John 5 is referring to Passover. That wouldn't make sense because Passover is spoken of by name throughout the Gospels. If it were Passover, John would have called it Passover. *Sukkot* is known as "the festival" (*HaChag*). In John 5:1, this word has no definite article "the"; it's "a Jewish feast." Of the three pilgrimage holidays, the only one not mentioned in the Gospels by name is *Shavuot*, or Pentecost. I believe that the holiday in John 5 is *Shavuot*, which means the Feast of Weeks, so called because it begins seven full weeks, or exactly fifty days, after the Feast of Firstfruits (two days after Passover begins). This understanding is vital to appreciating what is going on.

Several clues in the text hint that *Shavuot* is the holiday to which John was referring. John 5:2 says there are "five porches." What's significant about the number 5? Well, on the first *Shavuot*, God came down on Mount Sinai, gave the Torah to the people, and spoke the Ten Commandments (Exodus 20 and Deuteronomy 5). Ultimately, *Shavuot* is when Jewish people celebrate the giving of the Five Books of the Torah. The mention of the number 5 could be seen as symbolically related. Five is also the number for mercy and grace, which connects to the word *Bethesda*. This miracle happened on the day God gave the Torah, the Five Books of Moses, by His grace.

## God's Loving-Kindness

The pool's name is *Beit Chesed* (Hebrew) or *Bethzatha* (Aramaic). These names mean "house of loving-kindness or grace." The meaning is significant because, on *Shavuot*, Jewish people read the book of Ruth. The author of Ruth used the word *chesed* (kindness) in the story, which focuses on Boaz's kindness toward Ruth and Ruth's kindness toward Boaz. In the story,

Ruth was destitute. She needed mercy and grace, and Boaz offered her *chesed*. We also read Ruth on *Shavuot* because the story's events happen on *Shavuot*, which was founded on *chesed*, God's grace and loving-kindness. *Shavuot* is associated with *chesed* more than any other holiday.

God gave His covenant to Israel as an act of grace. *Chesed* is representative of God's covenantal love (Ex. 34:6–7; Num. 14:18–19; Ps. 17:7; 136). God entered into covenant with Israel at Sinai, which was symbolic of His covenantal love. So, *Beit Chesed* can mean the place of God's mercy and kindness. In this miracle in John 5, all these individuals were at two giant pools, most likely places for ritual washing (*mikvaot*). "When this site was excavated, it revealed a rectangular pool with two basins separated by a wall—thus a five-sided pool—and each side had a portico."[2] Fresh water from one pool fed the other (*mikveh*). But the name could also mean "place of shame or disgrace," so there's a double meaning here. The Lord's kindness transformed the paralytic—He took away the shame and disgrace the man felt. Yeshua, more than anyone, embodies the *chesed*, the loving-kindness, the covenantal love of God. He embodies the grace and mercy of God, who takes away our shame by His grace, as Boaz did for Ruth.

## The Secret Behind the Number 38

Remember, this man had been an invalid for thirty-eight years. We'll see that this number is essential to understanding this miracle. People probably thought the man was an invalid because he was a sinner. Yeshua challenged that thinking in an instant. But the question is, Why did He heal the man during this feast? Why on *Shavuot*?

Let's begin by examining the number 3. Scriptures tell us that three types of infirmed people were at the pool: blind, lame, and disabled (v. 3).

And Yeshua commanded the man to do three things: "Get up! Pick up your mat and walk" (v. 8). The Torah was given on the third day of the third month, through the thirdborn, and the *Tanakh*, the Hebrew Bible, is threefold: the Torah (the law), the Writings, and the Prophets. Everything connected to the giving of the Torah connects to the number 3. God said to Moses, "Be ready for the third day. For on the third day ADONAI will come down upon Mount Sinai in the sight of all the people" (Ex. 19:11).

Now let's look at the number 38. People often recount that the Israelites wandered in the desert for forty years (Deut. 2:14). Well, that's true and not true. Yes, they were in the desert for forty years, but thirty-eight years were because of their unbelief. They sent twelve spies to the Promised Land two years after they left Egypt. The people refused to obey God and enter the land because ten of the twelve spies reported that it was too dangerous to enter because of the giants there. Except for Joshua and Caleb, that generation died in the wilderness because of their unwillingness to trust God.

The Israelites could have arrived at the Promised Land in two years, but they spent thirty-eight years in the wilderness because of their unbelief. Yeshua essentially said in John 5, "Do you want to be healed and enter your promise by faith? Or do you want to be like the generation that died in the wilderness?" The number 38 is a numerical value of the Hebrew word *libo* ("his heart"). By asking the man if he wanted to be well, Yeshua tested him to see what was in his heart. The generation of the adults that came out of Egypt had such a slave-and-victim mentality that they kept testing God. Yeshua didn't want that to happen to this man.

John recorded this miracle partly to demonstrate that this victim mentality doesn't have to happen to us. There is hope if we believe and have faith in the greater than Moses, the Messiah, Yeshua. Yeshua healed this man, and He can heal us. We've seen many miraculous healings through our ministry. Once, I was speaking at a California church and said, "Listen, if anyone wants prayer for anything, including healing, come forward." A high school girl came forward and asked, "Can you pray for me?" She was on crutches and in a lot of pain with a torn ACL. She told us, "I'm a cheerleader. I want to believe that God's going to heal me. I believe God's going to heal me."

*Lord*, I thought, *did You have to make the first one so difficult?* Usually, when you pray for people, it's not about issues where you'd see an immediate response. Yet I could tell she came with such faith and expectation. After I prayed for her, she said, "Okay, let me put down my crutches." Two friends held her up, and she began to hop along. Then she began to walk along, and then she began to run through the place in no pain, praising God because He had healed her!

There can be a new normal in our lives. God's creative power and healing flowed through this man at the pool of Bethesda. He didn't have to die in isolation. Yeshua essentially said, "Do you want to be like the generation that came out of Egypt, who died after thirty-eight years? Do you want to die in this state? Or do you want to get up and walk and follow Me and obey?" Israel disobeyed, so they died in the wilderness. This man had to make a choice. So do we.

But of course, there is more here. The numerical value of the Hebrew word *chal* is 38. Hebrew words are built on a root of three letters. This trilateral root can be further broken down into a two-letter subroot. In the two-letter subroot of *chalah*, the Hebrew word for sickness is *chal*, which has a numerical value of 38. *Chal* also means "weak," which connects to sickness. This word is the root of the word for sick (*chalah*). The root of the word for sickness has a numerical value of 38. Interestingly, the word for disease (*machalah*) has the numerical value of 83, and 83 is the mirror image of 38. Abraham was circumcised at 99, and according to Jewish tradition, he offered his son as a sacrifice at age 137. ("Sarah was ninety when Isaac was born and Abraham was 100 years old [Gen. 21:5]. Sarah died when she was 127 [Gen. 23:1]—so Abraham would have been 137 and Isaac would have been 37."[3]) So there were thirty-eight years between the promise of the son, Isaac, and the offering of Isaac as a sacrifice. The more we look, the more we find to illuminate the brilliance of God's planning.

# Mount Sinai

On *Shavuot*, God not only gave the Torah; He did something significant for the people of Israel gathered at Mount Sinai: a miracle of healing. Immediately after leaving Egypt, the people of Israel were too physically weak to receive revelation from God—to receive the Word of God, the Torah. God made them wait fifty days because they still suffered the effects of Egyptian bondage. He was preparing them for what was to come next.

## The Healing at Mount Sinai

The Lord fed His people manna and quail, giving them water from the rock to nourish them. God renewed and strengthened them physically. But He also healed all their sickness, according to Jewish tradition and the rabbis. Healing and health preceded the giving of the Torah. Third-century Talmud scholar Rabbi Joshua ben Levi said, "When Israel left Egypt, there were among them men crippled by heavy labor, for as they worked in clay and bricks, now and then a stone, dropping from the structure, would break a man's arm or sever his leg. Hence the Holy One said: It is not right that I give my Torah to cripples. What did He do? He beckoned to the ministering angels, and they came down and healed them."[4] This angelic appearance is amazing because, in some versions of John 5, there was an angel that came down and stirred the water of the pool of Bethesda before the infirm would go in. And in Jewish tradition, an angel came down on Mount Sinai and healed all the people.[5] God healed the deaf—we know because Exodus tells us that everyone heard the voice of God (Ex. 20:1 THE VOICE). He healed those who couldn't walk—we know because everyone stood at Mount Sinai.[6] They all had to be able to stand. They all had to be able to hear the voice of God.

All the people of Israel saw the fire and the lightning and heard the thundering at Mount Sinai. The implication is that they saw the words of God as though God's word had a physical manifestation—as though the people supernaturally saw sound waves. In a sense, before their very eyes, they could somehow see the words that came out of God's mouth, the solidity of the words, as we see in the *midrash*. God healed them because they were entering into covenant with Him.[7] And this was not just for the generation standing there at the foot of Mount Sinai. Entering the covenant was for all generations. God didn't want anyone to say, "Well, I'm not a part of this covenant because my ancestor was blind, so he couldn't see what was happening at Mount Sinai," or "My ancestor was deaf, so he couldn't hear the voice of God," or "My ancestor was lame and couldn't stand before the Lord at Mount Sinai." Standing is the position of swearing an oath, giving testimony, or witnessing. The people of Israel had to be healed before the giving of the Torah. They were entering into the holy covenant, and with holiness comes healing.

## The Covenant at Mount Sinai

All of Israel had to be able to know what they were getting into with the covenant. They had to be in a place where they could meaningfully agree. God was going to appear to Israel in a spectacular way, but before this could happen, the people had to prepare themselves (Ex. 19:10–13).

All the people witnessed the thunder, lightning flashes, sound of the trumpet, and mountain smoking. And when the people saw it, they trembled and stood far off. They all heard, saw, and stood. God brought healing to the people before they received the Torah. This directs us to understand that the wisdom of the Word of the Lord brings both physical and spiritual life and blessing. As Proverbs says about wisdom, "She [wisdom] is a tree of life to those who embrace her, and blessed will be all who hold firmly to her" (3:18). This "tree of life" is traditionally understood to be the Torah. When Jewish people do their Torah service and read from the Five Books of Moses from the scroll, we recite that proverb when we place it back in the Torah.

Again, God did not want to exclude anyone from experiencing the event. He wanted to give His words to the whole people who were whole. He wanted it for everyone, not just for a few. This was a covenant that the Jewish people had been entering into for generations. All participated. *All* Israel mattered to God. God called *all* to be a holy priesthood in a royal nation. Priests who were not whole and had physical defects could not serve in the Temple. It's not that God discriminates against people with physical disabilities. It's that the Temple or the Tabernacle was symbolic of the Garden of Eden, and anything reminiscent of the curse could not enter. Sickness, death, and the brokenness in the world are a result of the Fall.

Remember, God healed every blind, deaf, and disabled person.[8] In a sense, God's coming down on Mount Sinai was a return to Eden. God was walking again amid the people. When God walks in our midst, there is healing. The same power that the Children of Israel experienced at Sinai was again revealed and experienced in the man's life at the pool of

Bethesda. Yeshua was manifest at Mount Sinai. God was even more manifest in the person of Yeshua when He became physically embodied in the incarnation. On the holiday of *Shavuot*, which celebrates the giving of the Ten Commandments on Sinai, Yeshua healed the paralytic at Bethesda, in an echo of the healing that occurred on Mount Sinai according to Jewish tradition.

## God's Healing Power

What God does, He wants to do again and again. In Hebrew the word for witness is *eid*, which shares the same letters as the Hebrew word for again. These things bear witness to what God wants to do again and again. We read about *Shavuot* in Acts 3:1–10. A lame man from birth encountered Peter and John about to enter the Temple. He was there to beg for money from people as they came and went. Expecting money, he looked at Peter and John. But instead of giving him money, Peter told him to "get up and walk" (v. 6). Peter and John wanted to give the man something greater than money. They wanted, by the power of Yeshua, to transform his life. Not only that, they could experience God's power working through them and could do greater works through that power.

This passage in Acts 3 connects to John 5:20: "For the Father loves the Son and shows Him everything He does. He will show Him even greater works than these, so that you will be amazed." Yeshua did as He saw the Father do. He healed the man on *Shavuot*, or Pentecost, and Peter and John followed in His footsteps, demonstrating the healing power of God on *Shavuot*. Acts 3 is a reenactment of Mount Sinai. Just as God healed on *Shavuot*, Yeshua healed on *Shavuot* because He's the greater than Moses. And then Peter and John followed in Yeshua's footsteps, healing on *Shavuot* because Yeshua had said, "Amen, amen I tell you, he who puts his trust in Me, the works that I do he will do; and greater than these he will do, because I am going to the Father" (John 14:12). God can use you in the same way as you follow in His footsteps.

## From Hopelessness to Healing

God wants to move you from hopelessness to healing. The key is faith and trust. But we must understand that faith is often fragile when we've been through years of affliction or hardship. Look what happened to the Children of Israel. They were slaves for hundreds of years. Millions of Israelites saw miracle after miracle—ten plagues in Egypt, the parting of the Red Sea, leaving with the wealth of Egypt, a supernatural provision in the wilderness, hearing the voice of God, seeing the fire, hearing the thunder, experiencing the greatest public revelation of God in history at Mount Sinai. And what did they do? They made a golden calf because Moses took too long to come down from the mountain (Ex. 32). They lacked faith and trust because of all the generations of hope deferred. They couldn't move completely from hopelessness to healing because they had a slave mentality that they acquired in Egypt. The Israelites experienced great freedom and healing at *Shavuot* but then lost it.

There are times when my faith and trust have wavered. What helps me the most is remembering God's faithfulness (His *chesed* as I wrote earlier). Also, I try to fall back on His promises. His Word is full of promises that, because of His faithfulness, we can rely on completely. I know He's faithful, I have faith in His promises, and I trust in His plan for me (Prov. 3:5–6). You, too, can move from hopelessness to healing by remembering His faithfulness and trusting and having faith in Him.

## Yeshua, the Great Healer

By healing the man at Bethesda, Yeshua showed that He's the greater than Moses. He showed that He is the Messiah. In Matthew 11:3–5, the disciples of John the Baptist said to Yeshua, "Are You the Coming One, or do we look for another?" Yeshua responded, "Go report to John what you hear and see: the blind see and the lame walk, those with *tzara'at* are cleansed and the deaf hear, and the dead are raised and the poor have good news proclaimed to them." We can find many prophecies about Yeshua's healing power in the Old Testament book of Isaiah. Isaiah 35:5 says, "The eyes of the blind will be opened and the ears of the deaf unstopped." Isaiah 42:6–7 says, "I, ADONAI, called You in righteousness, I will take hold of Your hand, I will keep You and give You as a covenant to the people, as a light to the nations, by opening blind eyes, bringing prisoners out of the dungeon, and those sitting in darkness out of the prison house." Coming "out of the dungeon" and "out of the prison house" describe the ability to walk and get out and find healing. Yeshua's healings were in fulfillment of messianic prophecies. They showed that Yeshua was the Great Physician, the Great Healer, and He still is today.

### Healing on the *Shabbat*

In John 5, when Yeshua healed the man, the religious leaders were upset because it was on *Shabbat* (the Sabbath). It's interesting how Yeshua responded. He openly declared His relationship with His Father and made it clear that He was doing His Father's work, not His own—and He would do it on the Sabbath or any day of the week. He responded to a person's need.

Why is healing on the Sabbath so significant? It wasn't just to give the Judean leaders an excuse to persecute Him. All this connects to the giving of the Torah on Mount Sinai. There are two opinions in Jewish tradition. Some say God gave the Torah on the sixth day of the week, which is Friday. Others say God gave the Torah on the sixth of *Sivan* (May-June), which happened to be a Friday, the sixth day of the week. The day God gave the Torah was a *Shabbat* or was just going into the *Shabbat* (a Saturday). Yeshua healed on the *Shabbat* just like God healed on *Shabbat* at Sinai according to Jewish tradition. Yeshua was saying in John 5, "Look, I'm the Son. I can only do what I see My Father doing." The Father commanded healing on the first *Shavuot*, the first Pentecost. So Yeshua also healed on Pentecost.

This is incredible. Yeshua said, "For just as the Father raises the dead and gives them life, so also the Son gives life to whomever He wants" (John 5:21). According to Jewish tradition, on *Shavuot* when the Israelites heard the voice of God, they were so overwhelmed by the power of God's voice, by the power of God's glory, by the overwhelming revelation, that they all died. Their souls left them, and God had to, in a sense, resuscitate them from the dead. It's as though Yeshua was saying, "Look what happened on the first Pentecost. I'm going to do that! I raise the dead just like My Father did. I am the resurrection and the life." Then He said, "Whoever hears My word and trusts the One who sent Me has eternal life. . . . Those who hear will live!" (John 5:24–25).

## The Voice of Yeshua

Yeshua speaking throughout the Gospels is like God speaking at Mount Sinai. Through the voice of Yeshua, we hear the voice of God—the voice that thundered at Mount Sinai. David wrote, "The voice of ADONAI is powerful. The voice of ADONAI is full of majesty. The voice of ADONAI breaks the cedars. . . . The voice of ADONAI hews out flames of fire. The voice of ADONAI shakes the desert. ADONAI shakes the wilderness of Kadesh" (Ps. 29:4–8). The voice of God comes with power. And we see this when Yeshua spoke. That same voice was speaking through Him. Remember when the soldiers went to the garden with the Pharisees to arrest Yeshua? When Yeshua identified Himself to them, saying "I am," "they drew back and fell to the ground" (John 18:6). The power in Yeshua's voice at the pool of Bethesda is like the power in God's voice at Mount Sinai.

## A New Covenant

Again, Yeshua said, "Whoever hears My word and trusts the One who sent Me has eternal life" (John 5:24). He was saying, "Just like there was a covenant at Sinai based on God's *chesed*, I'm making a new covenant." And just as Israel heard the word of God and had to commit to belief and obedience, so Yeshua was saying to the paralyzed man, "You must believe in My words and obey and enter into this renewed covenant, and then you will find eternal life. But if you don't, it won't go well for you." In His response to the leaders who were upset after He healed the man in John 5, Yeshua referred to Moses: "Do not think that I will accuse you before the Father. The one who accuses you is Moses, in whom you have put your hope. For if you were believing Moses, you would believe Me—because he wrote about Me. But since you do not believe his writings, how will you believe My words?" (John 5:45–47).

Yeshua connected His words to the words God spoke to the people at Mount Sinai. He said that the words the people heard at Mount Sinai were written about Him. Let's ponder this for a moment. The Lord healed all Israel at Sinai. The day was *Shavuot*, Pentecost. It was a *Shabbat*. God healed on the *Shabbat*. Yeshua healed on the *Shabbat* of Pentecost. The Holy Spirit came on Pentecost (Acts 2). The goal of the Torah, of all the commands, is to connect us to the Lord so that we can find life. Deuteronomy 4:4 says, "But you who held tight to ADONAI your God are alive today—all of you." And remember, Proverbs 3:18 says, "She [Wisdom] is a tree of life to those who embrace her, and blessed will be all who hold firmly to her." In the same way, we are to cling to God and hold tight to His Word. The Lord calls us to hold tightly to Yeshua, the embodiment of God and the living Word.

## Freedom

The healing in John 5 was not just for this one man. It also communicated a message to the religious leaders. Yeshua was saying to them, "Are you going to be like the generation who came out of Egypt? They saw the miracles in Egypt, they saw the miracles at Sinai, yet due to their unbelief, they died in the wilderness. Are you going to believe by faith and receive the promises and blessings that come through faith and trust in the Messiah?"

God's Word brings freedom! Exodus 32:16 says, "The tablets [the Ten Commandments] were the work of God, and the writing was the writing of God, engraved on the tablets." The Hebrew word for engraved (*charut*) is similar to the word for liberty (*cherut*). God's Word brings liberty, for there is no individual freer than one who occupies himself with the study of the Torah. And whoever occupies himself for the sake of the Torah is elevated.

## Believe, Obey, and Be Blessed

Yeshua revealed His glory and healing power on the same day that God revealed His glory and power on Mount Sinai to demonstrate His covenantal love and goodness. The religious leaders had to decide. When Yeshua confronted them with the choice to believe and be healed or remain stuck in the wilderness, it all happened at the sheep gate. In a sense, Yeshua was separating the sheep from the goats (Matt. 25:32–33). It's as though Yeshua was saying, "My sheep hear My voice. Are you going to hear My voice? Are you going to believe and obey? If you do, you'll find life." Yeshua healed the man at the pool. He was presenting this man as one of His sheep—spotless and blameless, in a sense, as a living sacrifice. He gave the disabled man a new beginning based on His grace and kindness. And yet the religious leaders accused Him of breaking the *Shabbat*.

Believe, obey, and be blessed. Joshua and Caleb entered the Promised Land because of their belief and obedience. Disbelief leads to disobedience, which leads to dismissal from the promises of God and the Promised Land. That's the generation that died in the wilderness because of a lack of faith.

## The Secret of the Number 11

What strikes me here is that the number 38 is made up of two numerals: 3 and 8. If you add 3 and 8 together, you get the number 11. You may be asking, "So what?" Interestingly, the Torah tells us that the journey from Mount Sinai to the Promised Land was supposed to be eleven days (Deut. 1:2). But the eleven-day journey turned into a thirty-eight-year wandering in the wilderness (two years at Mount Sinai and thirty-eight years wandering) because the people lacked faith. The number 11 can represent supernatural breakthroughs. The Israelites were not free until the eleventh miracle, the parting of the Red Sea, when God brought them through. Interestingly, Joseph of the Old Testament was the eleventh son, and, in his dream, eleven stars were going to bow down to him. His life centered on the number 11 and God's favor on his life. And in a sense, this man in John 5 was at the waters, waiting for them to stir in the same way God favored the Children of Israel and stirred (broke through) the waters at the Red Sea. But the lame man couldn't get in. Yet what's impossible with man is possible with God. Operating at the eleventh hour seems to be one of Yeshua's traits. This is what we find in John 2 with the miracle of the water into the wine. Remember, the miracle didn't happen until all the wine ran out—until we come to the end of ourselves and have no choice but to trust in Him.

## Enter into Your Healing

God doesn't call us to wander. When we try living in our own power and strength, we make our lives about religion, disconnected from a relationship with God. We become like those unbelieving Pharisees or the Israelites who died in the wilderness. The voice that spoke on Mount Sinai is the same voice that spoke the world into being. That voice and that word are the person of Yeshua. Man was not made for *Shabbat*; *Shabbat* was made for man, and it was made for our good—so, of course, Yeshua did good things on the *Shabbat*. And as a result, the healed man found life.

Yeshua wants you to find life and healing. You don't have to remain stuck. As He asked the man at the pool, Yeshua asks you, "Do you want to get well?" Then He says, "Pick up your mat and walk!" When you've lived with pain or sickness or in a place of trauma for so long, it's easy for hardship to become ingrained in your identity. You see things and interact in the world through that prism. It's hard to imagine life without that pain or sickness. But God says, "You know what? I've got more for you if you're willing to take the risk." He wants you to live by faith. He wants you to say, "I'm not going to be the one who dies in the wilderness. I'm going to be the one who enters the Promised Land." What say you? Will you persist in unbelief, or will you trust God and enter in?

## The Already Not Yet

When Yeshua began His ministry and started to proclaim the Gospel, the Kingdom began to break into this world. The supernatural reality of heaven became part of this natural world as it never had before. Because the Kingdom has come in a new and powerful way, healing and transformation are available to us. But we need to understand that the Kingdom came in part but not in whole. This means that we live in a tension between the present kingdom and the final Kingdom; healing and miracles are potentially available to us, but we may not always experience healing. Healing is possible and we should pray based on the finished work of Yeshua, but healing will not be fully manifested in our lives until He returns. Therefore, we should be hopeful for His healing but not lose heart or faith when He doesn't heal. Remember, God has a purpose for our lives that may or may not include healing in this present life.

# SIX

# THE SIGNS AND SECRETS
# OF WHOLENESS

As we continue our discussion about healing, let's examine the signs and secrets of the healing that leads to wholeness surrounding the nobleman's son in John 4. I realize we seem to be going out of order, but there are profound mysteries and secrets buried under the surface of this text that Bible readers don't usually unearth. Like Bethesda, one of the keys to this miracle's deeper truths is the meaning of the name of the place where the miracle occurred. We need to know why Yeshua performed this miracle at this location. If Yeshua did something somewhere and Scripture gives the place's name, there's a reason for it. And as we touched on in the previous chapter, we can't overlook the fact that we need healing before we can achieve wholeness.

Let's begin by looking at John 4:46–54. Yeshua returned to the Galilee and spent time with the Samaritans. He did some great things there, and many of them believed. That's what happens whenever Yeshua shows up and people experience His presence. He wants to visit all of us with His presence, spending time with us and doing great things as we seek His presence.

Yeshua returned to Cana of the Galilee, the same place where He performed the first miracle of turning the water into wine. A few verses earlier, the apostle John told us that people went out to greet Him. They had perhaps heard about or seen the miracles and signs (turning water into wine and the cleansing of the Temple) that Yeshua had done at the *chag* (the Hebrew word for feast). We've mentioned that this was likely the feast of Passover. That's the context here in John 4, as this noble-man, this royal official from Capernaum, came to Cana to seek Yeshua's help because his son was on his deathbed. He begged Yeshua to go to Capernaum with him, somewhere between fifteen and twenty miles away, to heal his terminally ill son. In those day they mostly walked or rode donkeys. Sometimes they took sailboats. Traveling that distance was quite a trek. But that was no problem for Yeshua, who spoke the word and miraculously healed this royal official's son from a distance.

## The Significance of Galilee

The details in Scripture are there for a reason. The first key detail of this account is that this miracle happened in Cana of the Galilee. Why did Yeshua perform miracles in this place? Some may think it would have made more sense for Yeshua to have done His miracles in Jerusalem, the spiritual center of the Jewish people. But the Messiah was raised in Galilee, not far from Cana. He did His first miracle in Cana. Most of His disciples were from Galilee, which became the base of operations for His ministry. According to Jewish tradition, the Messiah first had to appear in Galilee.

As we have seen in the Bible, names hold weight. The same is true with the name *Cana*. It alludes to essential mysteries concerning the identity and mission of the Messiah and the meanings of His miracles. Notice that every time Scripture mentions Cana, it says "Cana of the Galilee" (John 2:11; 4:46) or "Cana in the Galilee" (John 2:1; 21:2). When Scripture mentions Cana, it is in connection to the Galilee because it fulfills prophecy. As we read in John 1, Yeshua came to fulfill everything written in the Torah and the Prophets. One thing I'm looking forward to in heaven is sitting at the feet of Yeshua while He shows me the wonders in His Word of how all these things connect. So we must ask what prophecy He fulfilled by revealing His first miracles and messiahship in the Galilee.

The light of the Messiah, according to Isaiah, must first be revealed and shine in the Galilee:

> But there is no gloom to her
>> who was in anguish, as in time past.
>
> He treated lightly the land of Zebulun
>> and the land of Naphtali,
>
> but in the future He will bring glory—
> by the way of the sea,
>> beyond the Jordan—
>> Galilee of the Gentiles.
>
> The people walking in darkness
>> will see a great light.
>
> Upon those dwelling in the land of the shadow of death,
>> light will shine. (Isa. 8:23–9:1)

According to Isaiah's prophecy, the Messiah would come out of the Galilee region. Even Jewish tradition affirms that the Messiah would first appear in the Galilee.[1] Galilee would be the first to see the light of the Messiah, the great light that would shine in the darkness. Matthew 4:12–17 mentions that Yeshua is the fulfillment of Isaiah's prophecy:

> Now when Yeshua heard that John had been handed over, He withdrew to the Galilee. Leaving Natzeret, He came and settled in Capernaum, which is by the sea in the regions of Zebulun and Naphtali. This was to fulfill what was spoken through Isaiah the prophet, saying,
>
> "Land of Zebulun and land of Naphtali, the way of the sea, beyond the Jordan, Galilee of the nations—
>
> the people sitting in darkness have seen a great light, and those sitting in the region and shadow of death, on them a light has dawned."
>
> From then on, Yeshua began to proclaim, "Turn away from your sins, for the kingdom of heaven is near."

Yeshua as the Messiah had to fulfill all the messianic prophecies. This was to strengthen their faith, and ours.

## The Meaning of Cana

I believe that the Hebrew name for Cana (*Kanah*) provides insight into the mystery of why Yeshua began His ministry and performed His first miracles not only in the Galilee but specifically in Cana. The first mention of this place in Scripture is in Joshua 16:8: "From Tappuah the border went along westward to the Wadi Kanah and ended at the sea. This is the inheritance of the tribe of the children of Ephraim according to their clans." The Hebrew word *kanah* in this verse can be translated as "reeds." Yeshua did His first miracle in the place of the reeds because it is connected to another important messianic prophecy found in the book of Isaiah, which the Gospel of Matthew applied to Yeshua (12:15–21).

The apostle Matthew quoted Isaiah 42:1–4 to show that the Spirit-empowered Yeshua Messiah demonstrated He is God's chosen One. Through His many miracles, like turning water into wine and healing the official's son, He proved that He was the fulfillment of Isaiah 42. He was anointed and empowered by the Spirit to do signs, wonders, and miracles.

Isaiah 42:3 says, "A bruised reed He will not break. A smoldering wick He will not snuff out." The word translated "reed" is the same root word for Cana. We can interpret this prophecy from Isaiah to mean that the Messiah would be a humble individual who would not look to exalt Himself. He would shy away from conflict. The Messiah would be gentle and compassionate in His approach to people so that even a "bruised reed" the Messiah would not break. This demonstrates the loving, merciful heart of God. We can thank Yeshua for not breaking us. When we are hurting, we can pray something like, "My heart is heavy, Lord, yet I know You remember us in our lowly state and Your mercy endures forever. Thank You for remembering me in my frailty and brokenness. Thank You for Your enduring mercy. A bruised reed You will not break, and a smoldering wick You will not snuff out. I am bruised and smoldering, but my hope remains in You. I trust in You."

Yeshua cared even about the bruised reed. He demonstrated great care and concern for the lost sheep of Israel and the Gentiles of the nations, whom the religious leaders of His day did not care much about unless they converted to Judaism. It's no coincidence that in John 3, Yeshua focused on Nicodemus, a Jewish leader. Then in John 4, He focused on a Gentile official, who would have probably been the most despised of all these individuals by the Jews. It makes sense that He performed His first miracles in the city of Cana, which connects to a reed in Hebrew. He came to fulfill prophecy and bring hope and healing for Israel and the nations (Matt. 12:21).

There is another possible interpretation of "a bruised reed He will not break." Some understand these words from Isaiah to mean that the Messiah would not have to use great force for the nations to listen to His message, receive it, and believe in it. It would take so little force that even a bruised reed would not be broken in His bringing the message of salvation from the God of Israel to the nations. We see this in how the Samaritans (John 4:42) and the Gentile nobleman received Yeshua and believed in Him. He didn't have to argue with them, debate with them, coerce them, or threaten them with hellfire and brimstone. Initially, His message was received better by the Gentiles than by the Jews. This reality connects with John's writing: "He came to His own, but His own did not receive Him" (John 1:11).

Yeshua and the disciples knew the Greek and Aramaic languages, but Hebrew was their heart language, a holy language, and the language of Creation. This understanding of Hebrew means that Yeshua and at least some of His core disciples would have been intimately familiar with the nuances of Hebrew, such as the connection between Cana (*kanah*) and "reed." They would have understood these things as they read them and meditated on them over time. And these discoveries can bring just as much revelation and illumination to us today.

## A Connection to Creation

Yeshua did the first and second miracles in Cana, and we find out why in the Hebrew word *kanah*. Not only is it tied to Isaiah 42 with the bruised reed and the Messiah's anointing but it connects back to Creation itself. After Isaiah 42:3 says, "A bruised reed He will not break," it continues with, "A smoldering wick He will not snuff out." Then two verses later, Isaiah went on to say, "Thus says God, ADONAI, who created the heavens and stretched them out, who spread out the earth and what comes from it, who gives breath to the people on it, and *Ruach* to those who walk in it" (v. 5). This is mind-blowing to me! Why? The connection goes deeper than meets the eye.

We know the word *kanah* relates to the reed, which is the opening portion of Isaiah 42. But then the word also connects to God as Creator. The word *kanah* in Hebrew comes from what's called a trilateral root. As I mentioned before, most Hebrew words are based on a three-root system. In the word *kanah*, the first letter is *kuf* (ק), the second is *nun* (נ), and the third is *hey* (ה). When you read Hebrew, you must add the vowels yourself. If you open a traditional Torah scroll, there are no vowels. There are several ways a word could be read, depending on the meaning and context. The word spelled with *kuf, nun*, and *hey* could be read as *kanah*, which means "reed." But these same three letters can also be read as *koneh*, which means "creator." Genesis 14:18–20 says,

> Then Melchizedek, king of Salem, brought out bread and wine—he was
> a priest of El Elyon. He blessed him and said, "Blessed be Abram by El
> Elyon, Creator [*koneh*] of heaven and earth, and blessed be El Elyon,
> Who gave over your enemies into your hand."

The word for creator in these verses is *koneh*. This word is also found in Psalm 139:13: "For You have created my conscience. You knit me together in my mother's womb." The word "created" comes from the same root word as *kanah*.

In its root form, *Cana* connects to God and His work as Creator. He is the One who created the heavens and the earth. The first thing we read about Creation in Genesis 1:2 is that "the *Ruach Elohim* [the Spirit of God] was hovering upon the surface of the water." The first act of Creation involved God taming the waters and calling forth the light amid the darkness. In Yeshua's first miracle, the water into wine, He demonstrated He had control over the water. The miracle of turning water into wine connects to Creation. It is a new creation miracle—turning one thing into another.

## The Lord of Creation

The second miracle is also a creation miracle. That's why Yeshua did it in Cana. The healing of the Roman official's son alludes to Yeshua's identity as the Lord of Creation, which ties back to John 1:1–5:

> In the beginning was the Word. The Word was with God, and the Word was God. He was with God in the beginning. All things were made through Him, and apart from Him nothing was made that has come into being. In Him was life, and the life was the light of men. The light shines in the darkness, and the darkness has not overpowered it.

The apostle John's opening sentences connect to Genesis 1. Yeshua is the One who was in the beginning, who created everything that comes into existence. And He is the light that shines in the darkness—He did this day one of Creation. Remember, the first word of Genesis, *bereshit*, is usually translated as "in the beginning." We can also translate the phrase as "through the firstborn." Through the firstborn, God created the heavens and the earth. The apostle and rabbi Paul wrote, "He is the image of the invisible God, the firstborn of all creation. For by Him all things were created—in heaven and on earth, the seen and the unseen, whether thrones or angelic powers or rulers or authorities. All was created through Him and for Him" (Col. 1:15–16). This thought is critical because this miracle we are discussing revealed Yeshua's identity as not only the Messiah but also the Creator, God's firstborn.

## The Divinity of Yeshua

The book of John demonstrates that Yeshua is the divine Creator and Redeemer, which sets John apart from the other Gospels. John is unique in that it focuses on the divine origins and divine identity of Yeshua-Jesus. John's prologue does not deal at all with His natural birth but rather focuses on the fact that Yeshua existed in the beginning with the Father, is the agent of Creation, and is "the Word [who] became flesh" (John 1:14). The Gospel of John's unique use of the "I AM" statements further underscores its Christology that points to Jesus as the "Great I AM." Only Yeshua, who is the agent of Creation and in whom is found life, can have the power over death, even at a distance. That is why He was able to heal this man's son at the precise moment that He said, "Your son lives!" (4:50). This miracle demonstrated Yeshua's divinity and points to Him as the Creator. Only God has the power to bring life and bridge time and space. The royal official had heard about the miracles Yeshua had done. He wanted Yeshua to accompany him back to Capernaum, but Yeshua didn't go. Instead, He healed the man's son from fifteen to twenty miles away. This type of miracle was unheard of. In Yeshua's day, it would have demonstrated His incredible supernatural power and spiritual authority. He spoke the word, and it happened just as God spoke and the world came to be.

Usually, healing miracles, which were rare to begin with before Yeshua, involved the laying on of hands. This physical touching was the usual method by which Yeshua healed. Luke 4:40 says, "When the sun was setting, they brought to *Yeshua* all who were sick with various diseases. And He was laying hands on each one and healing them." Many passages in the Gospels mention healing in connection with the laying on of hands (Mark 6:5; 7:32; 8:25; Luke 13:13). But we need to remember that Yeshua is the One who does the healing—whether by speaking or by the laying on of hands. James, the brother of Yeshua, wrote, "Is anyone among you sick? Let him call for the elders of Messiah's community, and let them pray over him, anointing him with oil in the name of the Lord. The prayer of faith will save the one who is sick, and *the Lord will raise him up.* If he has committed sins, he will be forgiven" (James 5:14–15, emphasis mine).

However, just like with the nobleman's son, Yeshua still heals from a distance as well. I once prayed for a woman with diabetes over the telephone, and she was healed. Right after that, I spoke to the Promise Keepers staff and shared that story, and one of the men said, "I'm taking that for myself." When I saw him a few months later, he said, "You know what? That day that you told that story and prayed for people, I wound up getting healed of diabetes. I'm perfectly fine." Even now, you could be reading this and sense faith for healing rising up. Go for it! Today could be your day. Only the One who existed before space and time could heal at a distance, just as we see in John 4 with the nobleman's son.

As we mentioned in an earlier chapter, God doesn't always heal in this world's kingdom. Sometimes He asks us to endure, like the apostle Paul with his "thorn in the flesh" (2 Cor. 12:7–9). This "thorn" can cause us to draw closer to Him than we've ever been before. Sickness is rooted in the

Fall of Adam and Eve. Their sinful disobedience brought exile and sickness into the world. Every person inevitably lives with the consequences and effects of Adam and Eve's actions. Nations, communities, and individuals by faith and obedience can help minimize but can't completely mitigate the sickness and fragmentation that resulted from eating of the Tree of Knowledge of Good and Evil.

The Messiah performed miracles in Cana because Cana signifies the start of the new creation—the life and transformation He brought as the Messiah. That is one of the amazing secrets hidden in the Hebrew word for Cana, *kanah*.

## God's Decision and Solution at Creation

Let's return to the book of Genesis for a moment. Genesis 1:1 can also be translated as "God created on account of the firstborn." This means, you'll recall, that God created the world because the Messiah agreed to suffer and die for the future sin of humankind before the world was ever created. God knows the end from the beginning. He knew that man and woman were going to sin in the Garden. Before the world was ever created, before the Fall ever occurred, God decided and decreed the solution for sin. This is the meaning of John's words in the book of Revelation: "All who on the earth shall worship him [the beast]—everyone whose name has not been written from the foundation of the world in the Book of Life of the Lamb who was slain" (13:8). Before the world was ever created, the Lamb had already been slain, because for God, past, present, and future all exist simultaneously. God already decreed and decided that the Lamb was going to be slain. Yeshua died, in a sense, before the world ever came into existence.

## Creation and Redemption

Creation and new creation always begin with redemption. It should be no surprise, then, that the Hebrew verb *kanah* is used not only in connection to Creation but also in connection to redemption. *Kanah* is used to remind us of God victoriously redeeming His people. We read this in the exodus account where God parted the Red Sea: "By the greatness of Your arm they become still as a stone, till Your people cross over, *ADONAI*, till the people whom You purchased cross over" (Ex. 15:16). The Hebrew word for purchased in this verse is *kanita*. Exodus 15:16, talking about the redemption out of Egypt, says God purchased (*kanita*, from the word *kanah*) the Jewish people. Redemption is about acquisition.

The word *kanah* can be used when speaking of acquiring a field. Abraham purchased the field of Machpelah, where he buried his wife, Sarah (Gen. 23). This site became the tomb of the Patriarchs in Hebron. The word *kanah* is also used for acquiring a servant or a slave. The word appears in the context of Joseph being sold into slavery to the Ishmaelite traders (Gen. 37). It is also used in the narrative about Joseph buying "all the land of Egypt for Pharaoh" (Gen. 47:20).

We've seen that the word *kanah* has different meanings, but most importantly, it's used in connection to the messianic redemption: "It will also come about in that day that my Lord will again redeem—a second time with His hand—the remnant of His people who remain from Assyria, from Egypt, from *Pathros*, from Cush, Elam, Shinar, Hamath, and from the islands of the sea" (Isa. 11:11). So *kanah* is connected to the word for redemption in Hebrew. It is used regarding the redemption of Israel out of Egypt. *Kanah* is also used in Isaiah 11 when speaking of the messianic redemption: the Lord will redeem a second time. In the same way His hand redeemed people out of Egypt, the Lord's hand will redeem people through the Messiah.

In this and many other ways, it makes sense that the first two miracles of Yeshua happened in the place called Cana because *kanah* is connected to the redemption from Egypt. These miracles repeatedly show Yeshua as the greater than Moses. And as the greater than Moses, He will bring about the messianic redemption mentioned in Isaiah 11:11.

The term *redemption* can mean "to purchase out of slavery" or "to ransom,"[2] and it can be used in reference to the freeing of a slave from servitude. In Judaism, if a Jewish person had been kidnapped and sold as a slave, then it was a *mitzvah* (commandment of the Jewish law) to redeem him. The redemption that Yeshua offers us frees us from the forces that enslave us—first and foremost, the forces on a spiritual level. Sin creates a debt that we can't afford to pay. Yet sin demands a payment. Romans 6:23 says, "For sin's payment is death, but God's gracious gift is eternal life in Messiah *Yeshua* our Lord."

In the days of the Old Testament, when someone couldn't afford to pay his debt, he became an indentured servant to the one he was indebted to. The word *redemption* can mean "to buy back" and can be used for an individual redeeming another individual, like in the book of Ruth. Boaz is a type of messiah who redeemed Ruth. Ruth needed to be redeemed by her kinsman redeemer, her deliverer (*goel*). The same word is used of God redeeming Israel from Egypt. This idea forms the background of the New Testament understanding of buying a slave from an auction block. First Corinthians 6:20 says, "You were bought with a price."

The New Testament worldview sees our world as a place where humanity has become enslaved to sin, unrighteousness, death, and the forces of evil. But through Yeshua, we are offered redemption from the world, the flesh, and the devil's dominion and power. Yeshua "rescued us from the domain of darkness and brought us into the kingdom of the Son whom He loves. In Him we have redemption—the release of sins" (Col. 1:13–14). In Yeshua's first message in the synagogue in Nazareth, He proclaimed the year of Jubilee (Luke 4:18–21)—not a physical Jubilee where He released people from financial debt but a spiritual Jubilee as He freed us from our debt to sin. He paid our debt. We don't owe anything anymore. What great news! We don't need to be slaves to death, darkness, or sin. Yeshua is our Redeemer and we have been made alive in Him.

## The Bridegroom and His Bride

In addition to relating to Creation and redemption, the word *kanah* is also used in a Hebraic rabbinic context of a groom acquiring his bride. So *kanah* is connected to the Jewish legal term *kinyan*, a ritual and legal acquisition act. At a Jewish wedding, a groom must give his bride a ring. This act signifies that the groom is acquiring or taking her as a wife in a legal sense (*not* taking her as property). In "acquiring" her, he's making a legal and binding commitment to his bride. This goes back to Sinai, pictured as a wedding, a covenant, where God gave the Ten Commandments. When God gave the two covenant tablets, that was the means of acquisition. A wedding gift of monetary value symbolizes the seriousness of the groom's commitment to support and provide for his bride. How beautiful!

Yeshua began His work of acquiring His bride, the bride of the Messiah, at a wedding in Cana by performing His first miracle. He also performed His second miracle in Cana, a place whose name (*kanah*) relates to acquiring a bride. This miracle connects to John 3:29, where John the Baptist said, "The one who has the bride is the bridegroom, but the best man rejoices when he stands and hears the bridegroom's voice. So now my joy is complete!" It also connects to Revelation 19:7: "Let us rejoice and be glad and give glory to Him! For the wedding of the Lamb has come, and His bride has made herself ready." *Kanah* points to the Messiah's acquisition of us. There is always a price paid for the bride, and the Messiah paid that price for us. In the first miracle of turning the water into wine, "*Yeshua* . . . revealed His glory" (John 2:11). The Greek word for glory is *doxa*. In the book of John, *doxa* is always a reference to the cross. Yeshua's first miracle points to the glory of the cross—His death by which He purchased us. This connects to the Hebrew *kanah*. His second miracle points to the greater glory revealed through His resurrection. It points to life. The healing of the nobleman's son foreshadowed the resurrection life that we have in Yeshua.

## From Healing to Wholeness

We've examined this healing and some key words. Let's continue by exploring how healing moves to wholeness. John 4:46 tells us, "Now there was a nobleman whose son was sick in Capernaum." The Hebrew word for sick here is *choleh*. In Israel, a hospital is called the *beit cholim*, "the house of the sick ones." *Choleh* is singular for a "sick male," and *cholim* is plural for "sick people." There is rich spiritual and theological meaning in this term for sickness. This word in Hebrew at its root means "to make a hole" or "to hollow" or "to bore out." In Hebrew, sickness occurs when something is missing that should be there. This "something missing" is why sickness began at the Fall.

In the beginning, man was close with God, full of His life, presence, and glory. Man and woman cleaved to God and walked with Him in an intimate relationship. But sin entered the world when they listened to the serpent instead of the Lord. The result was separation on multiple levels—emotional, spiritual, physical, and relational. Sickness is a result of this separation. Sin leads to sickness because it creates a vacuum within man and creation. Man was whole in the beginning. Then man sinned and there was a disconnect between humanity and God, creating an empty void. This void became an opening for sickness and other corruptions of God's good creation. But a void begs to be filled.

## Filled with God and with His Good

"Now the earth was chaos and waste, darkness was on the surface of the deep" (Gen. 1:2). In the beginning, there was an empty space, a void, that chaos and darkness filled until God called forth the light of His presence on the first day. The chaos and darkness were overcome when God came into it. The first day's light was not the light of the sun and moon or the stars. The light on the first day was the light of God's presence filling the darkness.

Something must fill every void because nature abhors a vacuum. If God's good doesn't fill a void, something will fill it with the opposite. Every one of us has a void. If it is not filled with God, we begin to reach for unhealthy attractions and lies that promise fulfillment but end up enslaving and destroying. When we call on the name of the Lord, however, He begins to fill us with His Spirit. He fills that void, just like at the very beginning of Creation, when the Spirit of God was "hovering upon the surface of the water" (Gen. 1:2). In the same way the Spirit of God restrained and removed the chaos and brought order and life out it, He comes into us and deals with the chaos that is within us—the sickness within us—and begins to heal us and make us whole. Every believer has unredeemed parts of their life. Everyone is "holey"—we've got holes in our souls. There will be chaos, sickness, and unhealthiness if God does not come into those places where we have gaps and hurts.

The places unfilled by God inevitably lead us into sin on some level. If we don't fill the void with God and His good, the Enemy will fill it with something else. Some of those unhealthy attractions and lies that people tend to fill the void with are:

- food
- sex and pornography
- drugs and alcohol
- codependent relationships
- the pursuit of money or power

Some things we try to fill the void with aren't necessarily bad in and of themselves. However, when we pursue them in an addictive way to fill the void, it will always be unhealthy because God—and a relationship with Him—is the only One who can fill that void. If we don't deal with the vacuum within us, it becomes like a black hole; it sucks in everything in our path.

Yeshua said,

Now when an unclean spirit goes out of a man, it passes through water-less places looking for rest and doesn't find it. Then it says, "I'll go back home where I came from." And when it comes, it finds the house vacant, swept clean, and put in order. Then it goes and brings along seven other spirits more evil than itself, and they go in and live there.

And that man's last condition becomes worse than the first. So also will it be for this evil generation. (Matt. 12:43–45)

When you remove a demon, an evil entity, an undesirable trait, or an addiction from your life, something else needs to take its place. If your house (that is, your life) remains vacant, something else will take up residency in it. If whatever is unhealthy is removed, but the Holy Spirit—the presence of God and His good—doesn't fill you, then more ungodly, unclean, and harmful things will come and fill that space. It will be worse than it was before.

It's like someone who goes on an extreme diet. When the dieter severely cuts their calories, they get to a point where they are starving. But then they tend to go from eating very little to overeating because they deprived themselves of food for too long. In the end they gain back the weight that they lost. They failed to substitute an unhealthy habit with a healthy habit. God longs to fill the holes in our lives. We can look to Him as our healer and fill the void with wholeness in Him. As mentioned before, we can turn to His faithfulness, promises, and Word for comfort and for wholeness only He provides.

## Sickness, Exile, and Redemption

Sickness can be considered a spiritual problem with a spiritual root, whether physical or emotional. All sickness has its source in the Fall, but even in most of our lives, unhealthy decisions that we've made can cause it. The word for sick (*choli*), according to the rabbis, comes from the word *chol*, which means "profane" or "unholy." We can consider sickness unholy and profane only because it was never meant to be this way. We were never meant to suffer so, according to God's original plan in the Garden of Eden. Remember, in Hebrew, the term *chol* is related to the word for vacuum or emptiness. This implies a void of sanctity, a void of holiness that allows sickness to enter. It's interesting because the Hebrew word for health is *b'riut*. The word comes from *bara'*, which means "creation." God can replace the emptiness with Himself.

Please know that I'm not implying that all sickness is because you have personally sinned or are living in sin. Many godly people with the greatest faith suffer and become sick and even die. But ultimately, all sickness is caused by the Fall and the corruption of God's creation.

Now, though, I'd like to talk about sickness of the soul. *Choleh* means "to hollow out" or "to make a hole." Because of sin, there's a hole in our soul as humankind. If there's a hole in a boat, the boat will sink. Similarly, if a person has too many holes in their life, their life begins to take on water and sink. The hole is the removal of something that should be there—holiness, wholeness, and health. It connects back to sin, exile, and sickness. There is a one-letter difference between the words *exile* and *redemption* in Hebrew. The word for redemption in Hebrew is *geulah*, and the word for exile is *golah*. The one-letter difference is the Hebrew letter *aleph*. *Aleph* relates to God. *Alupho*, meaning "master of the world," begins with the letter *aleph*. Most of the divine names of God—*Adonai, Elohim*—start with the letter *aleph*. When we add the Hebrew letter *aleph*, it adds God into our lives, adding wholeness through redemption.

When God created the world, He made space to fill it. Think about the galaxies. There are billions of stars and eight planets in our solar system. It's incredible to think about how the world is full of stars and planets. God created that void to be filled. God's first commandment to man was to be fruitful, multiply, and fill the world (Gen. 1:28). This was

115

His first commandment because we're called to partner with God in the work of creation. He called Adam and Eve to fill the existing space. If we don't fill that space with godliness and godly seed (godly disciples) then someone else (the world, the flesh, the devil) will come along and fill that vacuum.

There's an absence of divine godliness in the world. It's like how the Bible describes Israel with no inhabitants—it becomes formless and void. God wants to fill the space of our lives. He wants us to fill the space we're living in by being fruitful and multiplying and filling in the world—whether by having physical sons or daughters or raising spiritual sons and daughters. If we don't make disciples, the Enemy will.

We overcome being soul-sick (the *choleh*, the hole) and exile by bringing back the *aleph*—by bringing back God. When we insert the *aleph* that represents God and brings godliness into our lives and this world, it transforms the vacuum. We need to take the land and master it internally and externally by expanding and filling it. This partnering with God is a key aspect of bringing redemption to the world. Our spiritual redemption does not negate physical reality. As one rabbi said, "The messianic redemption does not imply the negation or annulment of the natural order or the present reality of exile."[3] The goal is not to eliminate exile but to transform it into redemption. The Lord calls us to transform exile (*golah*) into redemption (*geulah*). We find this in the miracle of the water into wine—taking something ordinary and transforming it into something extraordinary. Exile is water into blood, the good into the bad, blessing into cursing, order into chaos, life into death. Redemption is water into wine, the good into the better, the cursing into the blessing. Sickness is transformed into health and wholeness. Death is transformed into life, which is the connection between this first and second miracle. Exile's full reversal will come when Messiah returns.

# Secular, Holy, and the Number 7

The word for sickness also connects to the word for secular. Six days of the week are secular and ordinary, but the seventh day is holy. Society becomes sick and enters chaos when we remove God from it. Secular is the opposite of holy. A secular society is sick because the culture has removed God, the moral foundations, and spiritual principles. I'm talking about extreme secularism—atheism and agnosticism that try to destroy the Judeo-Christian worldview and foundation. Just look around. Immorality and perversion are celebrated as good and normal, while actual good is called evil and hateful. Our culture is sick. "Woe unto them that call evil good, and good evil," warned Isaiah, "that put darkness for light, and light for darkness; that put bitter for sweet, and sweet for bitter!" (Isa. 5:20 KJV). We are there.

Don't be fooled, though. God's patience in judging sin does not mean He is tolerating it. He is serious about holiness and is dealing with wickedness. Throughout the Bible, God lets us know His feelings in various ways. One, as we've been discovering, is through numerical symbolism. Holiness is connected to the number 7. God created the heavens and the earth in six days, but He sanctified the seventh day. He infused it with holiness. The six days of the week are like the body; the seventh day of the week is like the soul. When you remove the soul of Creation—the holiness and the spiritual reality of the world—you're left with a sick, dead world. This connects to Yeshua's healing of the nobleman's son. John told us the miracle happened "at about the seventh hour" (John 4:52). The opposite of sickness is holiness. Let me be clear: I'm not saying that people are sick because they are not holy. I'm saying that sickness, especially spiritual sickness, is the opposite of wholeness and holiness. Yeshua released holiness and wholeness onto this child, and he became healed.

Holiness and healing are connected. There is no healing without holiness. *Holiness* ultimately means being conformed to the image and likeness of the Messiah. To the degree that we're not like Him is the degree that there is something unhealthy in our souls, because He is what we should aspire to become. He is the Holy One of Israel, and when we believe in Him by faith, He takes our dirty robes of unrighteousness and clothes us with His holiness and wholeness. And that holiness, that justification by faith, brings healing and transformation into our lives.

The number 7 also connects to the messianic age (the time that is all *Shabbat*). This world is like the six days of a week. When the Messiah comes, it will be the seventh day, the *Shabbat*, the rest, the messianic Kingdom (Mic. 4:1–4). Messiah healed at the seventh hour because holiness and wholeness is rooted in the Messiah and the messianic Kingdom, shown to us in the recurrence of the number seven.

The *midrash*—Jewish tradition—says this: "At the time of creation, it was at the seventh hour that He [God] blew into his [Adam's] soul. At the eighth hour, He [God] brought [Adam and Eve] into the Garden of Eden."[4] Just as God breathed into Adam at the seventh hour and he became alive and was given a soul, Yeshua breathed new life to this child's soul at the seventh hour. Only two things have the breath of God: the soul of man and the Word of God. In essence, the soul of man is holy. God calls us to be holy. We're made in the image of God, which is why there is a sanctity to life. It's the reason we are forbidden to murder. In the same way, God's Word is "inspired by God," or "God-breathed" (2 Tim. 3:16). There's a sanctity and holiness to the Word of God.

Seven is also the number of completion. God and His goodness completely healed the nobleman's son and brought wholeness to his life. Whatever void you're experiencing in your life—emotional, spiritual, relational, or physical—ask God to fill you. Ask Him to fill the holes in your body, spirit, emotions, mind, and soul and to bring healing. I pray that He will bring health and holiness in the name of Yeshua-Jesus, our Messiah. For those of you struggling with disease, I pray for you and the comfort only He can bring. I also pray for healing.

# The Number 49

There's healing and wholeness that only the Lord can offer. In Hebrew, there are often multiple ways to spell a word. As I mentioned previously, the Hebrew word for sick is *choli*. One of the spellings of *choleh* has a numerical value of 49, which is the numerical value of *golah*, the Hebrew word for "the exile." In Jewish law, when Israel was in exile in Egypt for all those years, they fell to the forty-ninth level of spiritual impurity—*tumah* in Hebrew. So 49 can be associated with exile. It's associated with impurity. The numerical value of the biblical phrase "not good" (*lo tov*) also equals 49. These are all negative aspects of the number 49.

However, the number 49 does have a positive connection in Hebrew. *El-Chai*, meaning "God of life" or "the living God," equals 49. "ADONAI will bring" equals 49. "Lamb" (*tali*) equals 49. "To the slaughter" equals 49. "The blood" (*hadam*) equals 49. And "Judah came" (*yaboi Yehuda*) equals 49. So what does this tell us when we connect all this with the number 49? The God of life (49) will bring (49) a Lamb (49) to the slaughter (49). We read this in Isaiah 53:7, a key passage in Scripture: "He was oppressed and He was afflicted yet He did not open His mouth. Like a lamb led to the slaughter . . . so He did not open His mouth." The blood (49) of the Lamb (49) gives us the power to overcome sickness (49) and exile (49) and all that is not good (49).

It's amazing to see how all these numbers connect! As icing on the cake, God's number 7 times 7 equals 49. How cool is that?

# The Shepherds of Israel and the Good Shepherd

There is a connection between a sick person (*choleh*) and the Messiah, and this is linked to the promise of the metaphor of the shepherds—the spiritual leaders of Israel—found in Ezekiel 34.

In verses 1–4, the prophet condemned Israel's leaders. He let them know they should have tended the "flocks" more faithfully. Verse four says, "You do not strengthen the weak [from the root *chalah*], heal the sick [*choleh*], bind up the broken, bring back the stray or seek the lost. Instead, you have ruled over them with force and cruelty."

## What Is God's Response to These Shepherds?

In verses 11–13 and 16 we find the Lord restoring His sheep. We discover the loving shepherd who goes after the sheep who are scattered to restore and care for them. Verse 16 says, "I will seek the lost, bring back the stray, bind up the broken and strengthen the sick. But the fat and the strong I will destroy—I will tend them with justice."

In verses 4 and 16 in this passage, the Hebrew word for sick has a numerical value of 49. How does this connect to the Messiah? The shepherds of Israel, who were bad shepherds, didn't care about the sick. But then God Himself said He would come and shepherd the people. God is the Good Shepherd. Ultimately, He's a different shepherd. When we look at the New Testament, we find the fulfillment of prophecy. When Yeshua came, He said, "I am the Good Shepherd. The Good Shepherd lays down His life for the sheep" (John 10:11).

There's so much shepherd imagery in Scripture that helps us understand Yeshua as the Good Shepherd who came to bring healing. David was a type or a prefiguration of the Messiah, and I can just see the young shepherd watching over his sheep in the fields, loving them, protecting them, guiding them to green pasture and fresh water. When a lion and bear threatened one, David cared so much that he risked his life to rescue it. This caring shepherd is Yeshua to us. In His parable of the lost sheep, Yeshua talked about a shepherd who leaves the ninety-nine sheep to go after the one lost sheep (Matt. 18:10–14). Moses was a shepherd, but, again, Yeshua is the greater Moses. David was a shepherd, but Yeshua is the greater David. He's the greater Redeemer. Yeshua is the greater King. He loves you and is willing to lay down His life for you as promised in Isaiah 53: "Yet it pleased ADONAI to bruise Him. He caused Him to suffer. If He makes His soul a guilt offering, He will see His offspring, He will prolong His days, and the will of ADONAI will succeed by His hand" (v. 10). In this verse, Isaiah was saying it pleased the Lord to "bruise" Yeshua, who willingly submitted to bear all our sins. His bruising (from the Hebrew root word for sickness, *chol*) gave us life eternal. Yeshua was the final sacrifice for sin and spiritual sickness. The Good Shepherd brings salvation but also wholeness.

## The Moses Connection

Again and again throughout these miracles, we see God proving that Yeshua is indeed the Messiah, the greater than Moses that was promised. It is so with this miracle of wholeness as well. In John 4, before the royal official with the sick son approached Yeshua, the people of Galilee "welcomed Him [Yeshua]. For they had seen all He had done at the feast in Jerusalem" (v. 45). This "feast" is the Passover. Yeshua's first miracle in John 2, the water into wine, connects back to Moses—with the first sign or plague upon the Egyptians when Moses turned the water into blood.

However, Yeshua didn't turn the water into blood; He turned it into wine. Why? Because He didn't come to bring death; He came that we "might have life, and have it abundantly!" (John 10:10). He was announcing that the healing and transformation of the Kingdom had come.

The miracle of healing the official's son connects to the last miracle sign Moses performed to free the Israelites, which was the death of the firstborn sons in Egypt. Exodus tells us that all the firstborns of the Egyptians died, and even the royal officials were not immune to the plague. Through Moses, Gentiles in Egypt experienced death and judgment, but through Messiah Yeshua, the royal official's son received life. Amazing! Pharaoh dishonored Moses, and his son died, but this royal official in John 4 traveled many miles to see Yeshua. The official didn't send a servant but went himself because he was concerned about his son—perhaps a firstborn son. By rejecting the word of Moses, Pharaoh rejected God. The royal official in John 4 accepted God's Word, honored the living Word, Yeshua, and found healing and transformation. It is a mirror image and a hopeful message about what the Messiah has come to do for us all.

## Miracles and Speech

At the heart of Passover's redemption is the power of speech. God told Moses, "Go to Pharaoh and say to him: This is what ADONAI says: 'Let My people go'" (Ex. 7:26). Moses had to deliver this message to Pharaoh, but Moses resisted by saying, "ADONAI, I am not a man of words—not yesterday, nor the day before, nor since You have spoken to Your servant— because I have a slow mouth and a heavy tongue" (Ex. 4:10). The Lord responded, "Who made man's mouth? Or who makes a man mute or deaf, seeing or blind? Is it not I, ADONAI? Now go! I will be with your mouth and teach you what to say" (vv. 11–12).

Moses used his mouth to speak the message. And then the people of Israel used their mouths to praise God in response to the great deliverance God brought them. God's great redemption to Israel through Moses is known as the Passover. In Hebrew, it is *Pesach*, which the rabbis say can be interpreted as *Peh Sach*, meaning "the mouth that speaks or converses."[5] The rabbis explain that in Hebrew, the word for Pharaoh (*Paro*)—the villain of the story who wouldn't let the Children of Israel go—can be understood as *peh ra*, meaning "evil speech or bad mouth."[6] Pharaoh is connected to evil speech, witchcraft, sorcery, negativity, defaming God's name, and disrespecting Moses.

God commanded the Children of Israel to commemorate and celebrate Passover every year by holding a Seder and telling their children about God's deliverance of the people of Israel. Moses instructed the people, "You are to tell your son on that day [Passover] saying, 'It is because of what ADONAI did for me when I came out of Egypt'" (Ex. 13:8). On Passover, the Jews are to use the power of speech and the mouth to tell our children what God did.

The Passover Seder happens in the Hebrew month of *Nisan*—the month of signs and miracles. You'll remember that Yeshua's miracle of turning the water into wine (John 2) most likely occurred in *Nisan*. This miracle of the healing of the nobleman's son also happened in *Nisan*. *Nisan* is the month of redemption. In Jewish thought, *Nisan* (the month of Passover and the retelling of the story of freedom from exile, which is also called *abib*) is more specifically associated with the mouth (Hebrew word *peh*) and speech. Every Hebrew month is associated with a different physical sense or faculty. The name *Nisan* means "miracle of miracles." It's associated on many different levels with speech and the mouth because our mouths and the power of speech are foundational and essential to experiencing miracles in our lives.

Creation, revelation, and redemption link to the power of speech. In Creation, God spoke the world into existence. In Israel's deliverance from Egypt, Moses had to speak to Pharaoh. We remember that redemption every year by using the faculty of speech—our mouths—to tell our children and our families what the Lord did for us. I can think of no more incredible legacy than for our children and grandchildren to sit around us and hear God's stories. On Mount Sinai, God spoke the Ten Commandments. Regarding the new covenant, we declare, proclaim, and preach the Gospel using our mouths. In John 4, we read that Yeshua, as the greater than Moses, healed the nobleman's son from a distance. Moses commanded death upon the Egyptians' firstborn sons, but Yeshua commanded *healing* by the power of speech. Yeshua's healing demonstrated that He truly is greater than Moses and came to bring about greater redemption.

## Faith of the Eye and Faith of the Mouth

There are two levels of faith. There is "eye faith" and "mouth faith." "Unless you all see signs and wonders," Yeshua said to the nobleman, "you'll never believe!" (John 4:48). Yeshua was talking to the crowd, not merely the nobleman. He was talking about the eyes. The people wanted to have eye faith. They wanted to be eyewitnesses. If their eyes saw it, then they would believe. That is true of many skeptics. Even Rabbi Paul said this concerning the Jewish people: "Jewish people ask for signs" (1 Cor. 1:22). Paul was saying that what was true in the days of Yeshua for many was still true in his day. And even to this day, it's true. Many Jewish people, like myself, come to faith because of a miracle or a supernatural experience. Not always, but sometimes, God obliges us if we are honest seekers. Like when Thomas said unless he saw the nail prints and put his finger in Yeshua's side, he would not believe. Yeshua didn't scold Him but told Thomas to go ahead and put his finger in His side. Thomas did and cried, "My Lord and my God!" Yeshua gave Thomas what he needed and then said, "Blessed are those who have not seen and yet have believed" (John 20:24–29 NIV). Yeshua did for me something similar when I didn't know who Yeshua was.

Before I came to Messiah, I was working in the recording industry in New York City with a lot of famous people. I would watch their lives and think, *Man, there has to be more to life than just this.* That really began my spiritual searching. I started studying with my rabbi at the synagogue where I had my *bar mitzvah* and grew up, and I really wanted a supernatural encounter with God. I was Jewish and also into New Age spirituality. I had no idea that Yeshua was Messiah. That thought wasn't even in my mind.

So, I got seriously into meditation and yoga. I would meditate for hours a day, and one day as I was meditating, my soul began to vibrate and left my body. As my spirit rose toward the ceiling, I could see my body down in my room. I continued up through the ceiling, through the clouds, and then ultimately into heaven. This was not a dream or vision but a genuine visit into the spiritual dimension.

In heaven, I saw a King high and lifted up on His throne, surrounded by a glorious light. As I observed the wonders around me, I felt the supernatural power of God pulsate through every cell in my body. My body vibrated and shook under the power of heaven. I felt an inexpressible state of euphoria. Every cell in my being began to come alive with the ultimate shalom. There was a love like warm oil moving through and around me like I'd never known. Trying to describe this encounter from the perspective of this life is like trying to feel something while wearing gloves. We don't have the sensitivity. But in this experience, I felt as though the gloves of my flesh had been peeled off and I was one with God and this King on His throne.

Instinctively, I knew the King was Yeshua. He looked at me and spoke telepathically to my spirit and I understood. He said, "Many are called but few are chosen." Stunned, I asked, "Am I chosen, Lord?"

"Yes."

I wanted to stay in that moment of love and peace forever, but the next thing I knew I was back in my body shaking under the power of heaven. I ran around praising God and shouting, "I'm called to serve! I'm called to serve!" But I still wasn't sure what all that meant.

I was given an experience by God's sovereign grace. He had His reasons, though I didn't understand. Before this experience I was spiritually fragmented. This vision led me to faith in Yeshua and the spiritual, physical, and relational wholeness only He brings. I'm still learning.

Scripture tells us that many who believed only had a "signs faith"—a faith that believes only after seeing a miracle. For many people, faith is about sight. The author of Hebrews wrote, "Now faith is the *substance* of things hoped for, the *evidence* of realities not seen" (Heb. 11:1, emphasis mine). In Numbers 13, we read about the twelve spies who explored the land of Canaan. Ten of the spies came back with a negative report. They saw giants in the land, and fear overcame them. Their belief—their faith—was based on tangible evidence. But their eyes deceived them. They saw the giants and fearfully said, "We seemed like grasshoppers in our eyes" (v. 33). They maximized the giants and minimized themselves. In the process, they minimized God. Remember that of the twelve, only two—Joshua and Caleb—had the faith to believe. This type of faith looks past the natural and trusts God no matter the situation or circumstances. This level of faith is true faith; it causes one to see through spiritual eyes instead of our natural eyes. This faith believes God can fulfill His promises against overwhelming odds, even defeating giants. When people believe only because they see, often their faith doesn't last. Eye faith can be good; God can use it. But mouth faith is much better.

God spoke of Creation before He saw it. There was darkness and chaos. Then God said, "Let there be light!" God used His mouth and spoke the good before He saw the good. The same is true for us. Before we can see it, we have to speak it. For a person of faith, seeing is not believing, but believing is seeing. This is deep Kingdom faith that moves mountains. Yes, there are giants. Yes, there are fortified cities. Yes, there are many crazy obstacles. But mouth (*peh*) faith is redemptive and creative faith that releases the Lord's power and potential.

Do you have the level of faith that believes God calls forth things that are not as if they already exist? Do you believe what God says even if you can't see it? Paul wrote, "For in Him all the promises of God are 'Yes.' Therefore, also through Him is the 'Amen' by us, to the glory of God" (2 Cor. 1:20). Everything God says will ultimately come to pass, regardless of how crazy or impossible it might seem. Moses had to speak the promise of redemption before he and the Israelites saw the signs and received redemption from slavery. After Moses told Pharaoh to let God's people go and performed supernatural signs to validate that God had sent him, things worsened for the Israelites. They suffered more as Pharaoh made them work harder and stopped giving them straw to make bricks. But the words eventually had their effect, and the people were set free. It came to pass. And in the same way, Jesus' word of healing went out and caused the son's healing in John 4. The redemption of Egypt connects to the mouth and relates to Yeshua healing the nobleman's son by just speaking the word. Yeshua is the Word through whom the world was created (John 1:1–5). God's creative power resides in and is made manifest through Yeshua. Those who believe His Word and receive Him as the Messiah become new creations and find abundant physical and spiritual life. They find wholeness and spiritual healing that comes from faith, trust, and His word.

## Faith in Yeshua, the Word of God

There are some practical lessons to be learned in this miracle, about how to experience wholeness in our lives. First, look at this man in John 4 whose son was dying. In desperation, he traveled a long distance in the heat to seek out Yeshua. When you cry out to God like that, looking to Him as your only hope, you show Him that you are entirely dependent on Him. This complete dependence on Him moves the heart of heaven.

I am a father, and my children are precious to me. Whenever I hear them crying, my heart breaks. Once, when my son Avi was little, he was sick and suddenly fell to the floor, turned blue, and went into a seizure. Thinking he was dying, we called 911, and I prayed. I had never cried out to God so hard in my life! The paramedics came, and while tending him, the seizure stopped, and his color returned. Still, they put him in the ambulance and took him to the hospital. A spike in his temperature had caused the seizure, but my son would be fine. Praise God! He answered our prayers. I'm convinced my desperation at that moment moved the heart of heaven.

The second critical lesson when it comes to receiving healing has to do with faith. Yeshua didn't do miracles in certain places because the people had no faith in Him. Faith is what connects us to God. It's how we access salvation. If you believe in your heart and confess with your mouth, faith taps into God's presence, promises, and power (Rom. 10:9). But it takes mouth faith to declare the promises of Scripture. There is power in the mouth (*peh*). Life and death are in the power of the tongue (Prov. 18:21). Don't speak the negative. Instead, declare God's promises over your situation and your circumstances. Don't agree with the lies, the liar, and the negative report. Yes, we take a doctor's negative report seriously. But we speak God's promises and healing over our lives and plead the blood of the Messiah over us. Remember, in Hebrew, 49 is the number of sickness, blood, and lamb. By faith, we declare with our mouths the promises of God over our lives, and we receive the promises through the blood of the Lamb. And we wait on Him. Sometimes healing and wholeness don't come as we expect. But God promises total healing in eternity.

## Walking in Obedience

The power of speech and faith allow us to tap into healing miracles, yet it also requires obedience. The nobleman in John 4 "begged" Yeshua "to come down and heal his son" (v. 47). He was a royal official and wasn't used to people saying no to him. But Yeshua told him, "Go! Your son lives!" (v. 50). He wanted the man to trust Him to heal his son. And as we saw earlier, Yeshua healed this man's son at "the seventh hour" (v. 52). The number 7 represents wholeness and healing.

In the last two chapters we've learned a lot about healing and wholeness. Healing can happen in both physical and spiritual ways. A deeper commitment to God leads to wholeness, which leads to a more abundant life (John 10:10). Our Abba Father deeply loves us. He wants us to experience physical healing, but more importantly He wants us to experience wholeness. In both chapters people were healed physically. That may or may not be happening for you today. But you can have so many blessings from God through wholeness. Both the man by the pool and the nobleman saw healing, but they also experienced wholeness.

_SEVEN_

# THE SIGNS AND SECRETS
# OF MULTIPLICATION

## "How Am I Going to Pay for This?"

Several years ago, I moved to California to pursue my ministry dream job—and was fired. Around this time, I attended a conference on healing, and Pastor Bill Johnson laid his hands on me and said, "You will wear many mantles like Joseph." God also spoke to my heart at this conference, saying, _Jason, you will go through a season of Joseph. I'm going to take you through the pits and the prisons to prepare you for the palace._ And then He said, _But all this is because there's a great move of God coming. It's not rooted in fear, but it's rooted in faith. It's rooted in miracles. I'm going to heal and transform people's lives. And I want you to pray for people because when you pray for them, you'll see people be healed and transformed._

It was an incredibly tough and stressful season. My second son had just been born, and I didn't know how I would provide for my family or pay the mortgage. I had no ministry position and no income. People around me were concerned, yet God was speaking to me powerfully. *Jason*, the Lord said, *listen to Me. You're going to speak in stadiums.* I told this to a few people and some of my family. They just laughed at me and told me not to tell anyone. Soon afterward, I met revival leader Lou Engle, whose ministry TheCall holds large prayer events across the country, and he became a good friend. One day he called me and asked, "Jason, how do you break the spirit of anti-Semitism?"

"It's Ruth and Boaz," I responded, and expounded a bit on Ruth and Boaz from my Jewish perspective—how Jew and Gentile can unite.

"You have to come to share this at TheCall Detroit conference!" he said.

Immediately I felt a peace, and I knew it was going to be epic. Then I felt the Lord prompt me with these words, *I want you to take a film crew with you to film in Detroit and watch what I'm going to do.* I knew it was God, yet I also knew I had no money. God continued as if He was winking at me: *Pay for a cameraman and hire some crew in Detroit, rent some hotel rooms, and do this filming of leaders.* It was crazy! "Lord," I said, "I'm so excited, but how am I going to pay for all this?"

I trusted God, took a leap of faith, and went to the event. After I'd shared the message of Ruth and Boaz, a former Muslim walked up onstage and took the microphone. "I came to this country as a terrorist," he said with great passion to the crowd of thousands, "and God got ahold of me. I encountered Yeshua and my eyes were opened. And He changed my heart. I went from hating the Jewish people to loving the Jewish people." He got down on one knee, looked up at me, and asked for my forgiveness for the hatred of the Arab people toward the Jewish people. I got down on one knee and said, "Listen, I'm sorry for any hatred on behalf of Jewish people and all the conflict."

"It is time for Ishmael and Isaac to come together," he said. When he said that, the Holy Spirit powerfully fell on that place. People were weeping as God miraculously changed people's hearts. The next day, a girl came up and said, "Look, I'm Lebanese. Israeli soldiers killed my grandfather. I've hated the Jewish people. I was so touched by what happened last night. Please pray for me to love the Jewish people." It was a decisive moment. Lou said this was one of the highlights of TheCall conference. What's incredible about it is that I had stepped out in faith without the resources. I had no idea what would happen.

This chapter centers on the mystery and the miracle of multiplication that we read about in John 6, when Yeshua fed a large crowd of people with five loaves and two fish. We will answer two essential questions that bring the relevance of this miracle into the twenty-first century and encourage your faith: (1) What is the significance of the five loaves and two fish? and (2) How does this miracle point us to a new understanding of Yeshua as the Messiah? In addition, we'll discover how the Hebraic Jewish context goes deeper into the story to give us incredible insights and practical application. I pray you'll see this miracle like never before. I hope that you come to know that what God did for the people who benefited from Yeshua's miracle, He wants to do for you.

## Yeshua Tests the Disciples

God tested me to see if I would have the faith to believe and obey, even though I couldn't see a natural way forward. In John 6:6, Yeshua tested His disciples. A large crowd was following Him because of the miracles, and they wanted to see more signs from Him. Seeing the large crowd, "Yeshua said to Philip, 'Where will we buy bread so these may eat?'" (John 6:5).

There were five thousand men (v. 10), which means there were probably about ten thousand or so when you included women and children. There was no natural way they could feed a crowd of that magnitude. When Yeshua asked Philip that question, Philip must've thought, *What? That's impossible even if we had the money!* He said to Yeshua, "Two hundred denarii aren't enough to buy bread for each to get a little bit!" (v. 7). Philip probably also thought, *Plus, there's no village around with that much food to buy.* They were out in the wilderness. Most of the towns around them had only one to two hundred people, and certainly not enough food to accommodate thousands at once. There's also a detail we read later that the grass was green (v. 10 MSG). It was Passover at the end of the season, which means people would have consumed the grain for the season, and according to Jewish law, they couldn't eat the firstfruits of the new grain until after the second day of Passover, after the priests offered the firstfruits of the harvest to God. Then Andrew, the brother of Peter, said, "There's a boy here who has five barley loaves and two fish—but what's that for so many?" (v. 9).

Why did Yeshua test the disciples in this way? And what's the connection between the test and the miracle of the multiplication? The first thing we need to understand is the context. This is around Passover, a time of remembrance when Moses led Israel out of Egypt into the wilderness. In John 6, the crowd was also in the wilderness, a rural area of the Galilee. What does that have to do with testing? Deuteronomy 8:2–3 says,

> You are to remember all the way that ADONAI your God has led you these 40 years in the wilderness—in order to humble you, to test you, to know what was in your heart, whether you would keep His mitzvot or not. He afflicted you and let you hunger, then He fed you manna— which neither you nor your fathers had known—in order to make you

understand that man does not live by bread alone but by every word that comes from the mouth of ADONAI.

The disciples were tested; the crowds were about to be fed from above as with the manna, and they would receive nourishing words from the mouth of Yeshua.

## Trusting God for His Provision

God tested Israel in the wilderness. They had no bread and no way to get it. How were they going to eat? Were they going to starve in the wilderness? Jesus tested His disciples in the same way God tested Israel. God also tests us for teaching and training. The word here for test comes from the Hebrew word *nisayon*, which connects through its root word to the word for a banner—*nasah*, meaning "to lift up." The testing lifts us up in the same way that a banner is lifted up. It doesn't break us down or beat us up. When we pass the test, we go to the next spiritual level of maturity. Jesus' testing taught His disciples to depend completely on Him to provide in the same supernatural way God did for His people in the wilderness.

One of the lessons that Yeshua was trying to teach the disciples was that you can't pass a spiritual test or solve a spiritual problem by natural means. It takes faith, letting go, and letting God solve it (Phil. 4:13).

## The Mystery of the Seven

Were the disciples going to learn to trust Yeshua and pass the test that most of the Children of Israel had failed in the wilderness? This is the mystery of the seven. There were five loaves and two fish, totaling seven. Rest, trust, and provision all connect to the number 7. How? Through the story of Israel. On five days of the week, Sunday through Thursday, when the Children of Israel were in the desert, God gave them manna, but the manna was good only for the day, and it became rotten and putrid if they tried to eat it the next morning. God instructed the people to collect enough for the day and not to keep it overnight. This instruction taught the Children of Israel that they must trust God for their daily bread. Then, on the sixth day, they needed to collect a double portion, one to eat on Friday and the other to eat on Saturday. On the sixth day, they had to keep the portion overnight and trust that it wouldn't rot and would still be fresh the entirety of the *Shabbat* day. They collected enough on the sixth day for the seventh day. Why? It's about rest and trust. God did not want them to work on the seventh day; He wanted them to worship and rest on *Shabbat*, so God gave them the double portion.

Forty years later, when the Israelites entered the Promised Land, the manna stopped, and God promised to give them early and late rains for their crops. He promised grass for their livestock and plenty of food. He also cautioned them not to worship idols, because if they did, there would be no rain (Deut. 11:13–17). They still had to trust and depend on Him to provide. It was a continual process.

The land of Israel is not like Egypt, where there's a natural overflow of the Nile River that creates rich soil. In Israel, God had to provide the perfect amount of rain for the right amount of food. Too little rain led to famine; too much rain also led to famine because it would destroy the crops. Because of this, the Israelites had to trust God. If they obeyed His commandments and faithfully followed Him, He would provide, and their storehouses would be full. The manna was used to test the Israelites to see what was in their hearts and prepare them for the day they dwelled in the Promised Land.

God also tested them with the sabbatical year when they entered the Promised Land. The Children of Israel could work in the fields for six years, but not on the seventh. That year, the sabbatical year, was known as the *shemitah*. During *shemitah* the farmers were not allowed to work the ground, which meant they had to trust God for provision. It's as if God was saying, "If you're faithful to follow My commandments and choose to trust Me, I will provide. As you trusted Me to provide manna in the wilderness, will you trust Me and work the ground for six years and rest for the seventh?"

Resting for a year requires great faith, and Israel, as a whole, never kept this commandment. That's part of why the Babylonians exiled Israel for seventy years in Jeremiah's days. For every sabbatical year they ignored, God sent them into exile. The Children of Israel were allowed to farm the Promised Land for six years, but every seventh year, or "Sabbath year," they had to allow the land to lie fallow (Lev. 25:2–7). The tribes of Israel neglected to keep seventy Sabbath years and it is for this reason that God allowed Israel to be exiled to Babylon for seventy years, one year for each of the years that they ignored (2 Chron. 36:20–21). The generation that went into Canaan mirrored their ancestors that had come out of Egypt but died in the wilderness for not trusting and obeying God. Most of that generation and their descendants who went in and took the land didn't keep the sabbatical year, so they didn't get to keep the land.

## The Number 7 and Trust in God

Let's take a deeper look at the number 7. The number 7 symbolizes trusting God to possess your promise in the face of the improbable and impossible.

God wants us to say, "I will trust You, God, and enter into Your rest so that I can possess my promise in the face of the impossible. I will trust You, no matter how crazy it seems." God told the Israelites that they would take the land from the giants (Num. 13–14). How were they going to take the land from the giants? By trusting Him. How could they not sow in the seventh year and still have food to eat? By trusting God.

How about you? Will you trust God? You'll never have the rest you desperately need until you abandon yourself to the One who cares deeply for you. Trusting Him leads to spiritual and emotional rest because you release fear and anxiety to Him and no longer have to carry it.

Faith moves us from the six days of working to the seventh day of rest. In the ancient Middle East, slaves worked for six years. We often work six days a week today and rest on the seventh. Not moving from the six to the seven keeps you enslaved in Egypt, enslaved to the natural realm, enslaved to fear, anxiety, and the world. Instead, say, "I am not enslaved. I'm moving from the six to the seven." The choice is yours. It's about trusting God.

When the Israelites went in to possess the land, seven kinds of Canaanite peoples lived there. God told the Israelites to go in and march around the walls of Jericho for seven days. On the seventh day, they marched seven times. Seven priests were holding seven shofars. After the seventh circuit around the city, the walls crumbled (Josh. 6). This battle was their first victory in the new land, centered on the number 7. The whole deal seemed improbable and impossible. The people of Israel must have been thinking, *Really, God? All You want us to do is walk around the walls seven times, and on the seventh day, seven times, and somehow, miraculously, the walls are going to come falling down?* Yes! That's what God asked. They obeyed, and God fulfilled His promise. God's message was, "Listen, trust Me, and I will give you rest from your enemies." They began to possess the promise through trust and rest.

## The Number 7 and the Miracle of Hanukkah

Seven also connects to the Jewish winter holiday, Hanukkah. Perhaps you are familiar with the story of Hanukkah, known as the Feast of Dedication. We read in John 10 that Yeshua Jesus celebrated this feast. The story of the first Hanukkah happened in the intertestamental period, approximately 160 years before the birth of the Messiah.[1] There was a wicked king by the name of Antiochus who came to power. He was a Greco-Syrian Hellenist and wanted to unite with Alexander the Great's empire and become the supreme emperor. After he conquered Israel, Antiochus tried to force the Jewish people to forsake the Torah, God's commandments, the holidays, and circumcision. He wanted to unite his people around the pagan Greek culture.

Antiochus ransacked the Temple and established an image of the pagan god Zeus. Then he offered a pig on the altar, completely defiling the Temple with the most unholy animal. If that wasn't enough, he sent his emissaries out to the villages commanding the elders and leaders to worship the Greek gods and forsake the Torah. During this time, a godly priest named Mattathias Maccabees lived outside Jerusalem. He took a knife, killed Antiochus's emissary, and proclaimed, "Whoever is for God and Torah follow me." He began guerrilla warfare against the most powerful military power of the day, and God gave them victory. The miracle of Hanukkah is about fighting and God delivering the many into the hands of the few. Without God's intervention, there was no way a ragtag bunch of guerrilla soldiers could have defeated Antiochus's army.

Another part of the miracle of Hanukkah concerns lighting, as you may know, and connects to the number 7. When the Maccabees went to the Temple in Jerusalem and rebuilt the altar, they wanted to relight the menorah, the seven-branched candelabra. However, they had only one cruse of oil, enough to last for one day. They trusted God and lit the menorah anyway, and a miracle happened. The menorah burned for eight days. God multiplied the oil so that it lasted for seven additional days. That's why Hanukkah is known as the Festival of Lights.

As we read in John 6, when Yeshua took the five loaves and two fish and multiplied them, it was a miracle with seven. A couple of chapters later in the book of John, Yeshua celebrated Hanukkah, the Feast of Dedication. The miracle of loaves and fishes gives us the same message as Hanukkah because it's about trusting God to multiply our meager resources to manifest His glory. In the end, it's all about revealing God's power, glory, and love to a lost and hurting world. By the way, the name of the wicked king, *Antiochus Epiphanes*, means "God manifest." God wasn't manifest in Antiochus but in the Maccabees who defeated him. I encourage you to trust God with your meager resources and watch what He does to manifest His glory.

Yeshua's miracle was even more significant than what happened during the miracle in the days of the Maccabees. For the Maccabees, the oil God provided was enough to last for seven additional days until they could get new oil. But when Yeshua did the miracle with the seven loaves and fishes, there were twelve baskets of leftovers—a sign pointing to the life of the messianic Kingdom. In that Kingdom, there's not just enough for each of us; there is more than enough. There is no diminishment with our God—only overflow!

God doesn't want us to have a poverty mindset. He will provide more than enough in every situation and circumstance you face. Having this new mindset is a crucial concept. Do you believe that with God, there is enough, and He can multiply what you have to more than enough? Believe it. God will multiply your talent, resources, and time—so you are satisfied with your lot and rejoice in blessing others. Seven is about supernatural multiplication as well as provision. This number and concept reveals even more, as we find another mystery of the number 7 in the Old Testament story of Joseph.

## The Number 7 and Joseph

It's no coincidence that during Hanukkah celebrations today, we read the Genesis story of Joseph (Gen. 37–50). Joseph was a dreamer, and his brothers were jealous of him. We know that wherever there are dreamers, there will be haters. Joseph's brothers stripped him of everything he had and then sold him into slavery. As I mentioned earlier, God told me I would go through a season of Joseph. What did that mean? I was stripped of all I had. But Joseph's future was in God's hands, and I had to trust mine was too.

After Joseph was sold into slavery, he prospered as a servant in Potiphar's house for a season. But then he was falsely accused, and Potiphar sent him to prison, where he stayed for over a decade. But God was right there with him. While in prison, Joseph interpreted the dreams of the cupbearer and the baker. Then Pharaoh had dreams that centered on the number 7: seven healthy cows, seven skinny cows, seven healthy stocks that people would use to make wheat and bread, and seven unhealthy ones. Joseph had the wisdom from God to interpret the seven: seven years of plenty, seven years of famine. Because Joseph understood the number 7, Pharaoh promoted him, and he began to possess his promise.

Seven is the number of fullness—complete blessing. The beautiful thing is that because Joseph had faith and trusted God, he had the resources in the seven years of famine. I believe today we are in a season where God wants to bring plenty before the real famine comes, and we need to ask for Joseph-type wisdom as Yeshua's brother James asked us to do.

### Testing in the Subtraction

Joseph's name in Hebrew (*Yoseph*) comes from the word *yasaf*, which means "to add." It points to the fact that God is the One who adds. When Joseph was born, Rachel, his mother, named him and said, "May ADONAI add another son for me" (Gen. 30:24). His name implies our unlimited potential for growth and blessing in the Messiah. God wants to add to us. He wants us to increase and grow, to be blessed and be a blessing. God is about both addition and multiplication. But sometimes subtraction must occur first. The pluses will come, but we also need the minuses to test us.

Testing changes our mindsets and prepares us to receive the multiplication of God's manifest goodness in our lives. There's almost always lack before abundance. Just as He tested the hearts of the Children of Israel, God wants to test what's in your heart. If you can't trust Him in the season of lack, you will not trust Him in a season of plenty. And He will not trust you with the resources in the good times. Too many people ask to receive God's blessing and vow to bless others. But once they acquire the wealth, they neglect to steward it in the way God designed for them to bless others. We all need to be careful. Yeshua provided more food than was required on that grassy hillside. When He does this kind of miracle for us, we need to be good stewards of all He has provided and use our good fortune to bless others.

No doubt, going through a season of subtraction, like Joseph in the pit and prison, is painful. Sometimes it's hard to rejoice with a friend in their season of addition and multiplication when we are going through the opposite. Still, we must overcome the temptation to be frustrated and jealous. How we respond to and celebrate the blessing in others determines how God responds to us. If we pass the test, seasons of subtraction often lead to times of triumph, spiritual peace, and multiplication (James 5:7–8).

### Stewarding God's Blessings

As the son of Joseph, the carpenter, Yeshua would have had the name *Ben Yoseph*, "the son of the one who is added to by God." At His first coming, Yeshua fulfilled the role of Messiah *ben Yoseph*, the son of Joseph, the Suffering Servant. Like the Old Testament Joseph, He went through rejections, pits, and prisons. Then, He was promoted to the right hand of the Father and became a conduit of blessing. Joseph was also able to become a conduit of blessing to Egypt and his brothers (Israel) because God had tested his heart and he proved humble. I believe God is looking for those types of men and women today. This kind of testing prepared the disciples' hearts for what we read in the book of Acts when people sold properties and gave the money to help those in need. They didn't hoard it but used it to feed the poor, expand the mission, and help the brethren. Their early testing trained the disciples' hearts to trust God and to be stewards of His blessing.

# Against All Odds

Seven is about trusting and resting in God to see His promises come to pass against all odds. There's no way that five loaves and two fish could feed over ten thousand people. There's no way a ragtag bunch of Jewish rebels could overcome the greatest powers of their day and then light a

SIGNS AND SECRETS OF THE MESSIAH

menorah that had oil to last one day but burned for another seven. God loves to work against the odds. There was no way Joseph could set himself free from the prison or correctly interpret Pharaoh's dreams. What's incredible is that this isn't just something God did in the past; it's something we've seen Him continue to do even in the present.

The menorah represents the presence and the divine empowerment of God, which connects to this phrase in Zechariah 4:6: "Not by might, nor by power, but by My *Ruach*!" In Hebrew this phrase has seven words (*lo bechyil valo bakocha kiy em beruchiy*). This alludes to the seven branches of the menorah and the miracle of the seven additional days of the oil during Hanukkah.

How does this connect to modern times? The founding fathers of the modern State of Israel chose a golden menorah with two golden olive branches on the sides for their nation's emblem. They chose this because they recognized that the birth of modern Israel was a miracle that defied all odds. It was an impossibility. They understood, even though some were not religious, that somehow God did it.

No people other than the people of Israel have been exiled from their land, scattered across the globe, lost their language, and then after 1,900 years, found the restoration of their nation and language. That's miraculous. Israeli Jews were outnumbered by the local Arab community two to one when Israel declared itself as a nation. On May 14, 1948, Israel officially declared statehood. Five Arab countries with five standing armies announced they would not accept the UN Partition Plan for Palestine, which stated that part of the land would be given to Israel and part to the Arabs living there. The Arab people rejected it. This event happened just three years after World War II ended, when Nazi Germany annihilated six million Jews during the Holocaust. Five armies invaded Israel: Egypt, Syria, Jordan, Lebanon, and Iraq. The secretary

144

general of the Arab League, Azzam Pasha, made the following statement via radio: "This will be a war of extermination and a momentous massacre which will be spoken of like the Mongolian massacre and the Crusades."[2] This was after the Holocaust! Pasha was saying to the Jews in Israel, "We're going to exterminate you. We're going to wipe you out. We're going to drive you into the sea." The invading Arabic armies were fully equipped with artillery, tanks, armored cars, and other supplies at the time of the invasion. Do you know how many cannons Israel had? Zero. Do you know how many tanks Israel had? Zero. Israel had a total of nine old airplanes. They were vastly outnumbered and completely outgunned. Yet, against overwhelming odds, God gave a victory to the modern State of Israel. Israel had the victory in its War of Independence. It was a miracle. Israel was a sovereign nation for the first time in two thousand years.

Then, in 1967 during the Six-Day War, the Arab armies were getting ready to invade Israel when Israel discovered their plan. They launched a preemptive strike, destroying all the Egyptian airplanes on the ground. Israel won the war in six days. Then they rested on the seventh. They trusted, and they rested. David ben Gurion, the first Israeli prime minister, who was primarily secular, said this: "In Israel in order to be a realist, you must believe in miracles."[3]

## Turning Little into a Lot

If you're going to be a realist, from the standpoint of a biblical worldview, you must believe in miracles. Just looking at the way the modern State of Israel came to be demonstrates how God loves to defy the odds. What He did for Israel, He wants to do for you. God can do a lot with your little.

Not only can the Lord add and multiply what you have, but He can also make it last. When the Children of Israel wandered in the desert, their clothes and shoes did not wear out, and their food and water did not run out (Deut. 8:2–4). When you give the Lord whatever is in your hands, He can do more than you could imagine. Will you release to Him your five loaves and your two fish? Most people won't. Instead, they're scared of losing what they have and they grip it tighter. We have to be careful. A lot can become a little if one lacks faith. On the flip side, it doesn't matter to God how little you have—He'll work with whatever you have. Just give it to Him. Don't focus on your lack; focus on the Lord.

## Multiplication Removes Reproach and Shame

God also uses His blessings to take away our reproach. The miracle of the multiplication of the oil removed the reproach that the Jewish people had suffered at the hands of Antiochus and the Hellenists. The miracle of the multiplication of the wine at the wedding of Cana took away the shame of the couple whose wedding it was. The miracle of the multiplication of the bread and fish was meant to teach the disciples to trust the Lord completely so that they might never be put to shame. If the disciples had really learned this lesson when He tried to teach it to them, they would never have denied Yeshua at the cross.

I want to declare to you right now that God can multiply your resources. I pray that God would increase your faith, that you would trust Him, and that you will believe that He is *Adonai*, the Lord your provider. Every promise in Him is yes and amen. Don't be like the Children of Israel in the desert who grumbled, who didn't have the faith to trust God. If you obey, God will bless you.

## Modern-Day Miracles of Multiplication

I have personally seen miracles of multiplication. I'll never forget one of our early Fusion Global events many years ago in California. We were partnering with a local community that had a passion for Israel. We didn't do much advertising for this event, and people didn't know about our ministry then. We planned a night of worship, teaching, and *Havdalah*—the ceremony for the end of the *Shabbat*—and we would have a meal together.

We ordered and prepared food for our meal, expecting a small group of about twenty-five to thirty people. As the night began, we quickly realized that the turnout was three or four times larger than we expected. We knew we wouldn't have enough food to feed all the people who came that night, and there was no time to pick up more food. Meanwhile, people just kept coming and coming and coming.

"God," a group of us prayed, "would You multiply the food like You multiplied the bread and the fish?" The event had brought in more than one hundred people. God answered our prayer and multiplied the food! Not only was there enough to feed everyone who came, but there was leftover food, precisely like the story in John 6. That's what God does. He's a good Abba Father, and He often shows up like that in our lives if we let Him.

On another occasion, we were doing our weekly Bible study at Fusion Hollywood, and a girl approached us. She was a struggling actress and didn't have enough money to pay her rent. She was alone and overcome with fear and anxiety, so we prayed for her. When she arrived home, she found hundreds and hundreds of dollars in cash, fanned out as if on display. It was an absolute miracle! Maybe God supernaturally multiplied the money she had, or perhaps He prompted someone to give her the money anonymously. Whatever the method, God did it. Multiplying the girl's money was a testimony to His faithfulness and goodness. If you are in a desperate situation like that girl, you can believe what God did to feed the multitude; He can do it for you as well.

## Multiplying the Bread

Why did the Messiah choose to perform the miracle of multiplication with bread and fish? You might say, "Those were probably the only two things the disciples could find at the time." Certainly, God could have caused the disciples to find other things, but the bread and fish were all part of God's bigger plan. Nothing ever takes God by surprise. He knows the end from the beginning.

But why *bread*? The Hebrew word for bread is *lechem,* which connects to redemption. You'll remember that Passover, or *Pesach,* celebrates Israel's redemption from Egypt and is also known in Hebrew as the Feast of Unleavened Bread, or *Chag HaMatzot.* It's the Feast of *Matzah,* or *matzot* in the plural in Hebrew.

*Matzah* symbolizes two things:

1. It symbolizes the bread of affliction—*Ha Lachma Anya.* It reminds us of the tasteless bread that our ancestors ate in Egypt and the slavery they endured.
2. It is also the bread of redemption. When the time of redemption came, God brought the Israelites out of Egypt in such haste that even their bread would not have time to rise. So, they ate unleavened bread—God transformed the symbol of enslavement into the sign and taste of redemption.

The bread of affliction and the bread of redemption also point to the comings of the Messiah. In the first coming, He came to suffer—He ate the bread of affliction for us. However, when He returns, we will fully taste the bread of redemption.

## Bread and the Number 90

From readings around Christmas, you may remember a prophecy about Jesus in Micah 5:1, which says, "But you, Bethlehem Ephrathah—least among the clans of Judah—from you will come out to Me One to be ruler in Israel, One whose goings forth are from of old, from days of eternity." Amazingly, Bethlehem in Hebrew is *beit lechem*. It translates to "House of Bread." Both David and the Messiah, according to the Micah 5:1 prophecy, had to be from the House of Bread. By being born in Bethlehem, Yeshua was born in the House of Bread—it's connected to His kingship.

Remember, Hebrew is alphanumeric—every Hebrew letter has a numerical value. The Hebrew word for king is *melech*, with a numerical value of 90. It just so happens that 90 is the numerical value of *manna* in Hebrew—*mon*. Ninety is the numerical value of *lamb* in Hebrew—*taleh*. Ninety is the numerical value of *redemption*—*geulim*. Ninety is also the numerical value of *tzadik*, which means "holy and righteous one."

What does this connection to 90 tell us? Yeshua is the greater than Moses, born in the House of Bread, who offers bread like manna (90) to show that He is the messianic King (90) who came as the Lamb (90) to bring about redemption (90) so that each of us might become a *tzadik*—a righteous saint (90).

After Yeshua multiplied the bread as part of the miracle in John 6, a crowd of people found Him. They demanded another sign to show He was the Messiah. They wanted a sign like the manna God gave to Moses and their forefathers in the wilderness (John 6:31). Yeshua responded, "I am the bread of life. Your fathers ate the manna in the desert, yet they died. This is the bread that comes down from heaven, so that one may eat and not die. I am the living bread, which came down from heaven" (vv. 48–51). Yeshua revealed Himself as the true manna—the true bread that comes from heaven. He multiplied the bread that symbolized manna (90) to show He is the *melech*—the King (90).

Not only does manna have the numerical value of 90, but according to Jewish tradition, the manna rained down on the Children of Israel in enormous proportions. The manna that fell for the Israelites measured sixty cubits in depth, which is the equivalent of ninety feet high! Even in Jewish tradition, the amount of manna that the Israelites received is connected to the number 90!

## The Ancient Blessing for Bread

In Jewish tradition, a blessing is said not only before eating bread at a meal but also after you have eaten the meal and are satisfied. This tradition comes from the biblical command in Deuteronomy 8:10. Many believers don't know about this. This blessing is known as *Birkat HaMazon*, the "Blessing after the Meal."

In the classic musical *Fiddler on the Roof*, the town rabbi is inquisitively asked, "Is there a blessing for the czar?" (The czar was the ruler of Russia, who persecuted the Jews.) The rabbi responds by saying, "In Judaism there's a blessing for everything!" He pauses for a moment, and then he says, "May God bless the czar and keep him far away from us!"

There's no specific blessing for the czar in Judaism, but the rabbi wasn't too far off. Jews have a blessing for *just about* everything! There are blessings to say when waking up in the morning, going to bed at night, seeing an amazing view, wearing a new garment, traveling, and even after going to the bathroom! There's a blessing for performing *mitzvot* (God's commandments) and for many situations and experiences in life. We should be saying blessings all through the day!

The primary purpose of these blessings is to help God's people keep Him in the forefront of their minds, gratefully acknowledging Him for everything He does. Even though these blessings (Hebrew *berakhot*) can be spiritually beneficial, the rabbis instituted them. God did not directly command them. However, there are two exceptions. The first is the blessing after the meal, from Deuteronomy 8:10.

In John 6, Yeshua took the bread and blessed it. But how did He bless it? For thousands of years Jews have said this blessing over bread: "Blessed are You, Lord our God, King of the universe, who brings forth bread from the earth." But there's a problem with this blessing. Bread doesn't grow on trees or in fields. How can we say God "brings forth bread from the earth"? Wheat comes from the earth, but people must work hard to turn it into bread. It must be harvested, ground, sifted, and prepared for baking. The process is elaborate and intricate.

The rabbis are aware of the nuances in the blessing. Some in the Jewish tradition believe that in the ancient past, in the Garden of Eden, bread grew on trees. They came to this opinion from part of the curse of the Fall when God said, "By the sweat of your brow will you eat food" (Gen. 3:19). The Hebrew word for food in that verse can also be translated as "bread." Some midrashic tradition believes the fruit of the Tree of Knowledge of Good and Evil that Adam and Eve ate was wheat in the form of bread. This blessing also looks forward to the messianic Kingdom as the rabbis tell us that once again bread will grow on trees through the redeeming work of Messiah.

When Yeshua was doing the miracle of multiplication, He was showing that He came to restore everything that Adam and Eve lost in Eden. He gave the people who witnessed His miracle a sneak preview of what was coming. The miracle points to the messianic Kingdom when we won't have to earn our bread by the sweat of our brow. At the Lamb's wedding banquet, we can taste and see that God is good (Rev. 19:6–9). It's interesting to note that the same Hebrew root for the word *bread* (*lechem*) is also the verb that means "to make war." The Hebrew words have the same letters, which is noteworthy because people war over bread, provision, sustenance, and finances.

In the messianic Kingdom, the Messiah will bring abundance and blessing. He will feed everyone without toil and hardship. He will bring *shalom*—peace. It should be no surprise that after Yeshua did this miracle of multiplication, the people in the crowd sought to make Him king— they understood the connection (John 6:14).

## Bread and the Sabbath

Yeshua multiplied five loaves and two fish. We've talked about the miracle's relation to the number 7. Let's tie it all together. The Sabbath is on the seventh day of the week. On *Shabbat*, we traditionally have two loaves of bread known as *challah*. One of the main reasons for having two loaves is that it reminds us of the double portion of manna that God gave the Children of Israel as they went into the *Shabbat*. Each day they could collect only one portion, and they couldn't store leftovers. But they gathered a double portion on Friday to have enough for Friday and Saturday (*Shabbat*). Because they're eaten on *Shabbat*, or the seventh day, the bread and the manna connect to the number 7. The number 7 is also connected to both holiness and *Shabbat*. The first thing God sanctified and called holy was the Sabbath, the seventh day. To sanctify or to make holy means to consecrate or set apart. When we dedicate or consecrate our lives to God, we will be blessed and multiplied as Yeshua multiplied the fish and bread.

## The Connection Between Bread and the Torah

Bread is associated with the Torah—the foundation of God's Word. Both Moses and Yeshua connected bread and the Torah. Earlier we looked at Deuteronomy 8:2–3:

> You are to remember all the way that ADONAI your God has led you these 40 years in the wilderness—in order to humble you, to test you, to know what was in your heart, whether you would keep His MITZVOT or not. He afflicted you and let you hunger, then He fed you MANNA— which neither you nor your fathers had known—in order to make you understand that man does not live by bread alone but by every word that comes from the mouth of ADONAI.

When Satan (*Hasatan*) tempted Yeshua in the wilderness, Yeshua quoted from Deuteronomy 8: "Man does not live by bread alone." This passage is about manna. A few verses later, we read, "So you will eat and be full, and you will bless ADONAI your God for the good land He has given you" (v. 10). Yeshua connected bread and the Torah.

## Physical and Spiritual Sustenance

What is the relationship between saying a blessing after meals and reciting a blessing before reading the Scriptures? And what does this have to do with bread in the miracle of multiplication? The connection between these two mandates from the Torah is *sustenance*.

In *Ethics of the Fathers* (*Pirkei Avot*), a collection of wise advice, the rabbis say, "If there is no flour, there is no Torah. And if there is no Torah, there is no flour."[4] Without God's provision of food, we would not have the physical strength to study Scripture or serve the Lord diligently. On the other hand, people are more than material beings. We are also spiritual beings. Our souls cannot grow and be nourished apart from the spiritual sustenance provided by the Word of God. And this is communicated to us by the Torah (Deut. 8:3) and by Yeshua's actions.

Interestingly, the tempter came to Yeshua in the wilderness and said, "If You are *Ben-Elohim* [Son of God], tell these stones to become bread" (Matt. 4:3). Yeshua, quoting from Deuteronomy 8:3, answered him, "It is written, 'Man shall not live by bread alone, but by every word that comes from the mouth of God'" (Matt. 4:4). Although most of us rarely miss a meal, we often pass up the opportunity to study God's Word. Without bread (food), people will physically die. Likewise, when there is a famine of God's Word, people die spiritually. The Torah is bread for the soul.

In Ezekiel 3:3, God told the prophet to eat a scroll that contained words from God. We, too, are called to consume God's Word so it can nourish our souls (*nephesh*). People have become spiritually anorexic because they are neglecting God's Word. Pastor and author Eugene Peterson wrote, "There is only one text for the creation of authentic Christian spirituality, and that is Scripture . . . Christian spirituality is in its entirety, rooted in and shaped by the scriptural text."[5]

God cares about our material and spiritual well-being. That's why Yeshua fed the people physically and spiritually. He provided physical food so He could feed them spiritually through His teaching. God's

Word is bread for life. It is our *sustenance*, even more than physical bread. Without a steady diet of Scripture, we will starve ourselves spiritually.

## Yeshua Is the Bread of Life

Moses brought the people the Torah, which is the foundation of the old covenant. Jesus' teachings became the foundation for the new covenant as the greater than Moses. He brought the true and deeper meanings of the Hebrew Scriptures. He showed that we need both the old covenant and the new. The new without the old is like a soul without a body—it's incomplete! We need the body and the soul to be who God created us to be.

God's Word is sustenance for the soul, and Yeshua is the "Word [that] became flesh" (John 1:14). We must feed on Yeshua and feed on His Word. One must eat of Yeshua, as Israel ate of the manna, to survive and thrive.

If the only thing you do is eat bread, you'll only survive—you'll never truly thrive. In John 6, after the miracle of the multiplication, the crowd followed Yeshua and questioned Him:

> They said to Him, "Then what sign do You perform, so that we may see and believe You? What work do You do? Our fathers ate the manna in the wilderness; as it is written, 'Out of heaven He gave them bread to eat.'"
>
> *Yeshua* answered them, "Amen, amen I tell you, it isn't Moses who has given you bread from heaven, but My Father gives you the true bread from heaven. For the bread of God is the One coming down from heaven and giving life to the world." (vv. 30–33)

In Jewish thought, the king is supposed to ensure that the people have bread. An example is in 1 Samuel 21:1–7 when David went to the *tabernacle* and the priest gave him the consecrated bread—the bread of the Presence—for his men to eat, which was prohibited. David was their leader and had been anointed as their future king. He had a responsibility to feed his starving men. Even the ancient blessing for bread alludes to this, as we saw in the last chapter: "Blessed are You, Lord our God, King of the universe, who brings forth bread from the earth." Yeshua is the fulfillment of this blessing. He is the bread that comes from the earth—that's the resurrection! He resurrected from the dead on the Feast of Firstfruits, and the firstfruit of a harvest is the new grain, from which bread is made.

## The Significance of Five Loaves

There's another interesting connection between bread and the Torah. Yeshua had five loaves and two fish. The five loaves allude to the five books of the Torah. And Yeshua is the foundation and the fulfillment of the Torah. He is the One Moses, whom the prophets spoke of when the Torah was written. One of the most important reasons the Torah was written was to point to the Messiah. Yeshua is the One Israel was waiting for. He is the Messiah.

Remember, Hebrew is alphanumeric. We write numbers with letters. The way that the number 5 is written in Hebrew is with the letter *hei*. The *hei* is the letter of divine grace and divine breath (Ps. 33:6). This concept is crucial because it signifies that the law and grace are not in contrast. They complement each other. Only two things have the divine breath. The first is Scripture (2 Tim. 3:16). The entire Word of God is God-breathed.

People also have divine breath. Genesis 2:7 says, "Then ADONAI

*Elohim* formed the man out of the dust from the ground and He breathed into his nostrils a breath of life—so the man became a living being." God's breath brought life. God's Word breathes life into us. We can't live without breathing in oxygen, and we can't live without breathing in God's Word, which is oxygen for our souls.

The divine breath releases God's creative power and potential to bring forth His promises in our lives. Both bread and breath are tied to life.

You and I need the breath of God, but if we want Him to breathe on us as He breathed on Abraham and Sarah and as Yeshua breathed on His disciples, we must surrender to Him. We receive His breath, in part, by studying the Scriptures. He renews, transforms, and empowers us with His Word. We ask the Holy Spirit—the breath—to breathe on us, but we also have to breathe in the Word of God. It's oxygen for our souls.

## Multiplying the Two Fish

We've seen that the bread represents kingship, the messianic Kingdom, and the Torah. But what is the significance of the fish in this miracle? In Judaism and the Bible, fish represent abundance, fruitfulness, and fertility. At Creation, the fish was the first thing God blessed and multiplied. "Then God blessed them by saying, 'Be fruitful and multiply and fill the water in the seas. Let the flying creatures multiply on the land'" (Gen. 1:22). Think about how many fish are in the ocean. They're like the stars in the sky. They can't be counted! So first, God blessed the fish.

In Genesis 48:16, Jacob said, "The Angel who redeemed me from all evil, may He bless the boys, and may they be called by my name, and by the name of my fathers, Abraham and Isaac. May they multiply to a multitude in the midst of the land." The Hebrew word for "may they multiply" in this verse is *veyidgu*. The verb at the root of "multiply" is the Hebrew word *dag*, which means "to fish."

In the Hebrew language, the Bible, and Creation, fish symbolize the multiplication of fruitfulness and abundance. The multitude that left Egypt and wandered in the wilderness grumbled about the food. They grumbled about the bread and complained that they didn't have the fish and garlic they had in Egypt. In His miracle of multiplication, Yeshua was making a *tikkun* ("correction") for the sin of Israel in the wilderness. He wanted to prevent the people from grumbling about their hunger. Moses couldn't provide fish in the desert. Once again, Yeshua showed He was greater than Moses by providing the bread *and* the fish.

In the Creation account in Genesis, God blessed three things: fish (1:22), humankind (1:28), and the seventh day, *Shabbat* (2:3). In Hebrew, the word for fish, *dag*, is made up of two Hebrew consonants: *dalet* (ד) and *gimel* (ג). *Dalet* has a numerical value of 4; *gimel* equals 3. The word *fish* has a numerical value of 7. In Yeshua's miracle of multiplication, there are five loaves and two fish—seven. We've seen the significance of seven. Fish is eaten on *Shabbat* because *Shabbat* is the seventh day of the week. Fish has a numerical value of 7 because it points to the blessing of *Shabbat*.

Like bread, fish also connects to the Torah. When it rains, it's common for fish to open their mouths and catch the drops as if they desperately need water, although they're immersed in water and surrounded by it. Fish symbolize people who thirst for every drop of God's Word. The rabbis say you can think of the Torah whenever you read the word *water*.[6] In the same way that our physical bodies can't go for more than three days without water, our souls can't live more than three days without the Torah. Therefore, Jewish people read the Torah publicly on Mondays, Thursdays, and *Shabbat* (Saturdays).

In the same way that fish need water to survive, we need the water of the Word to survive. God's Word is water to our souls.

During the flood in the days of Noah, the fish didn't die. Water saved Noah and his family. Moses and the people of Israel were also saved by going through the waters. Even during God's judgment, even when the world seems to be in chaos and destruction, we'll be saved if we are immersed in the water of God's Word.

## Fish and the Great Commission

We've seen how fish connect to fruitfulness, fertility, and abundance. However, fish are also related to discipleship and the Great Commission. In Matthew 4:19, Yeshua said to His disciples, "Follow Me, and I will make you fishers of men." Then in Matthew 28:19, He commissioned them to "go therefore and make disciples of all nations." The Great Commission is the fulfillment of the original blessing in Creation because God first blessed the fish.

God also blessed humankind at Creation: "God blessed them and God said to them, 'Be fruitful and multiply, fill the land, and conquer it. Rule over the fish of the sea, the flying creatures of the sky, and over every animal that crawls on the land'" (Gen. 1:28). The Great Commission is the fulfillment of God's original blessing and the first commandment—to be fruitful and to multiply and fill the earth. Early symbols for believers were the *ichthus*—the fish—because they connected to their mission and our mandate to be fishers of men. As you will see in John 21, just as Yeshua filled the disciples' nets to bursting with fish, God always calls us to help bring in a great catch.

Yeshua offers us abundant life and causes us to be and make disciples of all nations who know and follow the Torah. We can be fruitful and multiply and raise up spiritual sons and daughters. If we don't raise up spiritual sons and daughters, the Enemy will. Yeshua said to His disciples, "Go therefore and make disciples of all nations, immersing them in the name of the Father and the Son and the *Ruach ha-Kodesh*, teaching them to observe all I have commanded you. And remember! I am with you always, even to the end of the age" (Matt. 28:19–20). Yeshua commanded His disciples to observe *all* His commandments. So, discipleship isn't only about salvation. It's about teaching people to walk according to God's Word. It's the bread, and it's the fish.

## Fish and the Messianic Kingdom

Fish is one of the healthiest foods you can eat. It's packed with low-fat, high-quality protein and vitamins such as D and $B_2$. It's also an excellent source of omega-3 fatty acids and other nutrients that help keep our hearts and brains healthy. And it tastes delectable! There's nothing like sitting down for a perfectly prepared fillet of salmon or tilapia, maybe a nice strip of bass or trout.

Fish also connects to the messianic Kingdom. In Jewish tradition, one of the main foods that will be served at the messianic banquet (*Olam Ha-Ba*, the World to Come) is fish. More specifically, Jewish tradition teaches that the great sea creature called the *Leviathan* will be eaten in the messianic era.[7] Fish is traditionally eaten on *Shabbat* because it points to the messianic Kingdom—*Shabbat* is meant to be a taste of the messianic age. When we eat fish, it reminds us that we're going to eat fish at the wedding banquet of the Lamb (Rev. 19:6–9).

## The Bread and Fish Together

A whole world is hidden from the naked eye under the water, under the seas. Fish represent the hidden identity of Yeshua and the concealed messianic aspects of His teaching.[8] Many religious leaders and others didn't understand His message and therefore didn't believe He was the Messiah.

Shortly after performing this miracle of the multiplication, Yeshua was in the synagogue, probably on the *Shabbat*, the seventh day, and He said to them, "I am the bread of life. Whoever comes to Me will never be hungry, and whoever believes in Me will never be thirsty" (John 6:35).

Let's look at the numerical puzzle pieces in this passage and in the miracle of the multiplication and discover a deeper meaning. The phrase *Halechem hachai* means "bread of life." The numeric value of the word for *Halechem* (bread) is 83, and *hachai* equals 23. These words total 106. The bread of life that Yeshua called Himself equals 106. The Aramaic word for fish, *nun*, also equals 106. Of the same value is one of the names of the Messiah from the Psalms—*Yinnon*. In multiplying the bread and the fish, Yeshua showed He is the messianic King.

The number 106 is also the numerical value of the following Hebrew phrases: *heemin*, "one who believes"; *halechem hachai*, "bread of life"; and *davak*, "to cleave" or "to hold tight." Deuteronomy 4:4 says, "But you who held tight to ADONAI your God are alive today—all of you."

In Matthew 11:28–30, Jesus said, "Come to Me, all who are weary and burdened, and I will give you rest. Take My yoke upon you and learn from Me, for I am gentle and humble in heart, and 'you will find rest for your souls.' For My yoke is easy and My burden is light." Jesus' "yoke" (*ulo*) in these verses is His teaching. And the numerical value of *ulo* is 106.

The number 106 is also the numerical value of *lavod*, "to serve";

*bekhol-levavkha*, "with all your heart"; *beyad melekh*, "into the hand of the king"; *hamelukha*, "the Kingdom"; *habigdei levan*, "white garment"; and *nun*, "fish."

Let's put this all together: Those who believe (106) that Yeshua is the bread of life (106) cleave (106) to Him and take His yoke (106). Those who follow His teachings serve (106) the Lord with all their hearts (106) and commit themselves to the hand of the King (106). These people will inherit the Kingdom (106), be dressed in white garments (106), and eat fish (106) at the wedding banquet of the Lamb! So, fish (106) connects not only to the bread of life but also to the Kingdom. They point to the abundance that we're going to experience when we cleave to Yeshua and love Him with all our hearts. When we place our two fish (106) into the hand of the King (106), God transforms them and multiplies them. He becomes the bread of life for us.

## God Uses What Is in Our Hands

We can apply to our lives what we have learned about Yeshua's miracle of multiplication and the significance of the bread and the fish. First, we can't solve problems by purely natural means. It was good that the disciples cared about the people and wanted to help meet their physical needs by feeding them, but they came up with only five loaves and two fish! Too often, we try to solve significant problems with our meager resources, apart from God. We see a need, and we think we can meet it on our own. But our meager resources can't solve life's significant problems.

We must bring every situation and big decision to God and trust Him. The more we rely on God and not on our wisdom and experience alone, the more God will multiply what's given to us. It's also important to understand that God will use what's already in our hands. The disciples had five loaves and two fish, and Yeshua performed the miracle with what they gave Him. God will bless what you have in your hand if you give it to Him and ask for His blessing, even if it's only a little bit of oil, a staff, or five loaves and two fish. God cares about the needs of His people. Yeshua cared compassionately about the hunger of the people. And because you know He cares, you can trust the Lord to meet your needs. No matter your situation and circumstances or how complex the problem is, will you give Him what you have? Put it into His hands. Then, trust and listen.

Wealth and honor and strength come from the Lord. I pray that God will bless you just as He did the hungry crowd with the miracle of the loaves and fishes. Have faith. Trust God. Give generously. And watch what He does.

# EIGHT

# THE SIGNS AND
# SECRETS OF SIGHT

Years ago, when I lived in North Carolina, I visited a friend in the hospital. As I left, I saw a woman standing outside, crying. People were walking right past her, ignoring her. I stopped and asked, "Ma'am, what's wrong? What's going on? Is there something I can do to help you?" She said, "My son is here in the hospital. He's dying of cancer. And it just seems like nobody cares. My pastor hasn't come. The chaplain hasn't spent much time with us, and I'm so distraught and sad. I don't know what I'm going to do." I said to her, "I'm a messianic rabbi. I'm Jewish, and I believe in Yeshua as the Messiah. Can I pray for you?" I prayed for the peace of God and the healing of God on her son. Then she wiped the tears from her eyes and said, "I'm so grateful because people kept passing me by. Nobody seemed to care. You're the only one who took the time to stop."

That's what I love about Yeshua. He didn't keep walking past people when He saw they were in need. He always stopped to help the hurting and needy because compassion moved Him. He helps restore our sight to help us also see others who are hurting or in need. Yeshua's compassion is evident in the healing of the blind man in John 9.

## Challenges of Blindness

In this miracle, Jesus stopped to help. The text says, "As *Yeshua* passed by, He saw a man who had been blind since birth. His disciples asked Him, 'Rabbi, who sinned, this man or his parents, that he should be born blind?'" (John 9:1–2). The fact that this man had been blind since birth adds to the dramatic nature of this miracle. It's hard enough to be blind in our modern times with all of today's technological advancements that assist the visually impaired. Still, blind people can do amazing things, have fulfilling careers, and live well on every level in our society. Being blind in ancient times, however, was a genuine hardship. It meant you were a poor beggar and societal outcast. The rabbis said that blindness, like leprosy, was comparable to death.[1]

Adding insult to injury was a commonly held belief by religious Jewish people and pagan Romans that disabilities and diseases were the results of either one's sin or the sin of one's parents. Deep shame was another factor. In addition, the Jews often assumed blindness resulted from idolatry or not offering animal sacrifices in the prescribed manner. The blind man in John 9 had been in his condition since birth, which is why the disciples asked Yeshua whether this man or his parents had sinned.

# The Historical Context

Jews in ancient times believed that a child could sin in the womb. Think about Jacob and Esau—they fought in the womb (Gen. 25:22). In rabbinic tradition, it's taught that when Rebekah was pregnant with Jacob and Esau, if she walked past a place where idols were worshiped, Esau would kick "and struggled to get out."[2] Though it's not in the Scriptures, it's in Jewish tradition, which gives some insight into how people thought at that time. Understanding the cultural and historical background helps us see the story in high definition and understand why the disciples thought the man's blindness could be the result of sin.

## Generational Sin

If this blind man was not guilty of iniquity, what about his parents? Was the man suffering due to generational sin? And even more importantly, can our children suffer because of the sin of our ancestors? Since this was and still is a commonly held belief, it's worth examining from a theological and scriptural point of view. This idea of generational sin— that God punishes the children for the sins of the parents—is connected to the Ten Commandments in Exodus 20:5–6: "For I, ADONAI your God, am a jealous God, bringing the iniquity of the fathers upon the children to the third and fourth generations of those who hate Me, but showing lovingkindness to the thousands of generations of those who love Me and keep My *mitzvot*." In Hebrew, "bringing the iniquity of the fathers" is *pokeid avon avot*. The interpretation of this passage depends on the definition of the Hebrew word *pokeid*. We can translate it two ways. The first and most common translation is that *pokeid* means "to visit," and some translations interpret this to mean that God punishes, or "visits" the children with punishment, for the sins of the fathers for up to three or four generations. When generations walk in the same sinful ways as their ancestors, they incur additional guilt. The traditional Jewish view of this interpretation is that it refers only to the sin of idolatry—not to other sins—based on the context of where it occurs in the Ten Commandments.

The problem with this interpretation is it seems to contradict other passages of Scripture, such as Deuteronomy 24:16: "Fathers are not to be put to death for children, and children are not to be put to death for fathers—each one is to be put to death for his own sin." And we also read something similar in Ezekiel 18:20: "The soul that sins, he will die. The son will not bear the iniquity of the father with him, nor will the father bear the iniquity of the son with him. The righteousness of the righteous will be on him and the wickedness of the wicked will be on him."

Since Scripture interprets Scripture, and Scripture can't contradict itself,[3] there must be a better way to understand Exodus 20:5. The rabbis found a solution to this contradiction by making a distinction between people who sin intentionally by consciously choosing to walk in the sins of their ancestors and those who choose the good way of truth by forsaking the way of their fathers. So, only the ones who intentionally choose a different path from their fathers are released from experiencing the consequences of their ancestors' sin. The judgment and the consequences build up for generations. The only way to avoid generational sin's consequences is to intentionally walk in the opposite direction. This solution has a certain logic, but I still find it unsatisfying. It doesn't seem to fully resolve the tension and the apparent contradiction with verses like Deuteronomy 24:16 and Ezekiel 18:20.

Consequently, we need to do a bit more digging to discover what this means.

## The Significance of the Character of God

What is even more bothersome about this interpretation is that it seems to run contrary to the character and nature of God revealed in the Scriptures. While Moses was on the mountain in the presence of God, receiving the tablets of the Ten Commandments, the people of Israel sinned by committing idolatry. This is the sin addressed in Exodus 20:5. Yet Moses pleaded for God to forgive them, and the Lord heard his prayer. The following words are in response to Moses' plea as he hid in the cleft of the rock:

> Then ADONAI passed before him, and proclaimed, "ADONAI, ADONAI, the compassionate and gracious God, slow to anger, and abundant in lovingkindness and truth, showing mercy to a thousand generations, forgiving iniquity and transgression and sin, yet by no means leaving the guilty unpunished, but bringing the iniquity of the fathers upon the children, and upon the children's children, to the third and fourth generation."
>
> Then Moses quickly bowed his head down to the earth and worshipped. He said, "If now I have found grace in Your eyes, my Lord, let my Lord please go within our midst, even though this is a stiff-necked people. Pardon our iniquity and our sin, and take us for Your own inheritance." (Ex. 34:6–9)

God's response in this chapter does not seem to be consistent with the first and more common interpretation of Exodus 20:5. The Hebrew word *pokeid* does not have to be interpreted in the sense of punishing the children up to the third and fourth generation. The same word *pokeid* is used in Genesis 21:1: "Then ADONAI visited Sarah just as He had said, and

ADONAI did for Sarah just as He had spoken." The word visited in this verse is the word *pokeid* and it means "remembered." Genesis 50:25 says, "Then Joseph made Israel's sons swear an oath saying, 'When God takes notice of you, you will bring my bones up from here.'" In this verse, "takes notice" is the word *pokeid*. Joseph said, "When God remembers you."

## God Remembers and Is Patient

Ibn Ezra, a historically significant rabbi and commentator, believed that the word *pokeid* in Exodus 20:5 should be translated as "remembers," not "visits."[4] Even though the Lord is jealous and hates idolatry, He is gracious and long-suffering, allowing the sinner to live. The Lord wants to give the individual and His children a chance to repent and change their ways. But suppose there is no change among an ancestral line after four generations? In that case, He serves judgment because the Lord does not just remember individual sins but those of their ancestors. I believe this translation is preferable—this is the opposite of the commonly held interpretation. It's not that God punishes up to three and four generations for the fathers' sins; it's that God remembers and waits for those generations to repent. Then, finally, He says, "Okay, enough is enough. You're not changing. I've been patient with you. I've given you generations to change your ways, yet nothing is changing."

I believe this is made clear in Genesis 15. The Lord appeared to Abraham (then Abram) in what is known as the Covenant Between the Parts, and He reaffirmed to Abraham that God was going to give him the land of Canaan, which was home to several pagan people, such as the Amorites and the Jebusites. Genesis 15:13–16 says,

> Then He [God] said to Abram, "Know for certain that your seed will
> be strangers in a land that is not theirs, and they will be enslaved and

oppressed 400 years. But I am going to judge the nation that they will serve. Afterward they will go out with many possessions. But you, you will come to your fathers in peace. You will be buried at a good old age. Then in the fourth generation they will return here—for the iniquity of the Amorites is not yet complete."

Why would God make His people wait four hundred years before they could inherit the Promised Land? We find the answer in Genesis 15:16: "For the iniquity of the Amorites is not yet complete." Israel went to Egypt and endured four generations of oppression because God was gracious and compassionate toward the Amorites. He gave the idolatrous and immoral peoples of the land of Canaan—including the Amorites— four generations to repent. But they didn't, and when their sin reached its full measure, God judged them through the Children of Israel. Israel began to expel those nations from the land. This judgment was according to God's promise to give the Israelites the land.

This second interpretation of Exodus 20:5 is preferable because it aligns better with the revealed character of the Lord. The Lord never wants to judge—this is always His last resort. God is patient. As we see in Genesis 15:16, a tipping point occurred after three or four generations, and judgment was inevitable because of the idolatry that permeated the Promised Land. The following passages describe the nature of God in this way:

ADONAI is gracious and compassionate, slow to anger and great in loving-kindness. (Ps. 145:8)

You are a God of forgiveness, merciful and compassionate, slow to anger, and abounding in love. Therefore You did not abandon them, even when they made a cast image of a calf for themselves and said, "This is your god who brought you up from Egypt!" or when they committed great blasphemies. (Neh. 9:17–18)

Rend your heart, not your garments, and turn to ADONAI, your God. For He is gracious and compassionate, slow to anger, abundant in mercy, and relenting about the calamity due. (Joel 2:13)

Exodus 20:5 communicates the exact opposite of what the disciples thought it meant and what many people still think it means—the idea that a person's sickness is the result of his or her own sin or generational sin.

Parents' sins can affect their children and their children's children. The natural consequences of a parent's actions influence the children. For example, if a woman is a drug addict and pregnant, her child could be born with challenges. That's a natural consequence. Suppose someone is born into a dysfunctional family where there is abuse. In that case, the person's suffering is not the Lord's punishment for a sin committed by their parents or one of their ancestors. It's the natural consequence of being born into a sinful environment.

Scripture—including Exodus 20:5—reveals that the Lord is not angry and vindictive like the false gods of the people who inherited the Promised Land. The God of Israel was utterly different from the pagan gods. The Lord is gracious and compassionate. He's not capricious and spiteful, but He's slow to anger. He doesn't want to punish but withholds complete judgment for some time. God's slowness to anger is good news about who He is!

We must be careful not to take the idea of "four generations" too literally. This time frame is a general principle about God's character and how judgment works. Peter explained this in 2 Peter 3:9: "The Lord is not slow in keeping His promise, as some consider slowness. Rather, He is being patient toward you—not wanting anyone to perish, but for all to come to repentance." The Lord's character always remains consistent. God said, "For I am ADONAI. I do not change, so you, children of Jacob, are not consumed" (Mal. 3:6). This is significant. God's people were not "consumed," or destroyed, because the Lord is immutable—He is unchanging. Hebrews confirms this: "*Yeshua* the Messiah is the same yesterday, today, and forever" (13:8). This is good news!

### God Is Considerate

So in the phrase "bringing the iniquity of the fathers" upon later generations (*pokeid avon avot*), we can interpret *pokeid* to mean that God *visits* the iniquities (punishes) or *remembers* the iniquities and withholds punishment out of grace. Yet there is another interpretation. According to German Orthodox rabbi Samson Raphael Hirsch, we can also interpret *pokeid* as "takes into account."[5] Based on this interpretation, when the Lord makes a judgment, He considers or "takes into account" every factor in our lives, including our painful pasts, upbringing, and what we have inherited emotionally, spiritually, and genetically. In other words, the Lord takes into consideration the damaging impact of our parents, our environment, and the negative inheritance we receive as children from them. This interpretation also aligns with what I believe is the better interpretation of *pokeid* as "remembers." This interpretation is more consistent with the revealed character and heart of God.

This line of thinking and interpreting Scripture is fantastic news! God knows everything every individual has been through. He knows all the pain we've experienced, all the hurt we've felt, and all the negatives in our lives that hold us back or handicap us in some way. God considers all those things when He looks at our lives and deals with us accordingly.

You don't have to be a victim of your heritage. You have a choice through the grace and power of Yeshua to break the strongholds of your family's past. You can't do it yourself, though. It will take a supernatural miracle, but that's what God specializes in and what this book is all about. Yeshua was raised from the dead, and He can raise you from a dead life of generational curses to new life in Him. However, if you were raised by an addict or were in an abusive situation, you've been exposed to that behavior and influence. You may even be genetically inclined to go that way. We live in a broken and cursed world. Still, we can be new creations in Yeshua, where He can heal our past and break generational strongholds. This, I believe, is part of what God wants to reveal to us in the miracle of the healing of the blind man.

## The Works of God Brought to Light

In the case of the blind man in John 9, Yeshua corrected His disciples in their view that the blind man experienced his disability due to some specific sin. "*Yeshua* answered, 'Neither this man nor his parents sinned. This happened so that the works of God might be brought to light in him. We must do the work of the One who sent Me, so long as it is day! Night is coming when no one can work. While I am in the world, I am the light of the world'" (vv. 3–5).

Yeshua affirmed that neither this man's sin nor his parents' sin caused his blindness but that "this happened so that the works of God might be brought to light." So, how does this miracle demonstrate the works of God? It validated Yeshua's message that He is truly the promised Messiah spoken of in the *Tanakh*, the Hebrew Scriptures. This man who was born blind was ostracized, and everyone believed he was suffering because of his or his family's sin. Yet Yeshua turned it around to glorify God and demonstrate that He is the Messiah. He can redeem and heal and transform every situation and circumstance.

That's what God wants to do in your life and the lives of your family and friends. Maybe you're dealing with guilt and shame in your life. Perhaps you're telling yourself, *I've brought this on myself. I deserve this.* The Lord says, *No!* Yeshua came to bring healing and wholeness. No matter what you've been through, your situation and circumstance, whether people judge you wrongly or you messed up. Sure, you may be suffering the consequences, but what you're experiencing is an opportunity for the works of God to manifest in you. And if you are still breathing, it's never too late. That's the beautiful thing. That's the good news!

## The Sign of Blind Eyes Opening

Yeshua's signs and miracles always validated and reinforced His message. The prophet Isaiah wrote that in the coming Kingdom, when God redeems the world, "Then the eyes of the blind will be opened and the ears of the deaf unstopped. Then the lame will leap like a deer, and the tongue of the mute will sing. For water will burst forth in the desert and streams in the wilderness" (35:5–6). German communal leader Rabbi Shimon Schwab commented on this passage and how it refers to the messianic redemption:

> During the [exile], our eyes are often closed to the [divine providence] of the Holy One Blessed be He. . . . And during the long [exile] we are often deaf to the exhortations to [repentance] and the promises of our eventual [messianic redemption] by the prophets. However, with the

coming [messianic redemption], our eyes will be open, and will see God's personal intervention in our redemption. And the words of the prophets, which for so long failed to penetrate our ears, will finally be heard and understood by us.[6]

The rabbi said that our eyes are often blinded as we await the Messiah's return. The man in this miracle was born blind. But the religious leaders were also blinded. They couldn't see that this miracle was part of God's divine plan and providence. Many people are often blinded and deaf to what God is doing. Why? Because of the pain of life and its challenges. The hurts we face frequently hinder our ability to see correctly. But as the prophet Isaiah wrote, one of the signs of the coming of the Messiah is that "the eyes of the blind will be opened" (35:5) to see God's hand involved in our situations and circumstances. God said to His people,

I, *ADONAI*, called You in righteousness, I will take hold of Your hand, I will keep You and give You as a covenant to the people, as a light to the nations, by opening blind eyes, bringing prisoners out of the dungeon, and those sitting in darkness out of the prison house. (Isa. 42:6–7)

Luke 7 gives us some context for how God's people were looking for signs of the coming of the Messiah:

When [John's disciples] appeared before [Yeshua], the men said, "John the Immerser sent us to you, saying, 'Are you the One who is to come, or shall we look for another?'"

At this very hour He was healing many of diseases, sicknesses, and evil spirits; and He granted sight to many who were blind. And answering, He said to them, "Go report to John what you saw and heard: the blind see, the lame walk, those with *tzara'at* are cleansed, the deaf hear, the dead are raised, and the poor have good news proclaimed to them. Blessed is he who is not led to stumble because of Me." (vv. 20–23)

If people were looking for signs, these miracles more than proved Yeshua was the Messiah.

## The Numerical Significance in the Miracle

The Hebrew word for "the blind man" (*ayin-vav-resh*) has a numerical value of 276: *ayin* equals 70, *vav* equals 6, and *resh* equals 200. Amazingly, 276 is the numerical value of one of the key names of God, *Adonai Tsidkenu*, which means "the Lord our Righteousness" or "the Lord is our righteousness." This is significant because there are only two places in Scripture where this name occurs, and both are key messianic prophecies:

"Behold, days are coming"—it is a declaration of ADONAI—"When I will raise up for David a righteous Branch, and He will reign as king wisely . . . He will be called: Adonai our righteousness." (Jer. 23:5–6)

I will cause a Branch of Righteousness to spring up for David, and He will execute justice and righteousness in the land . . . this is the Name by which He will be called: ADONAI our Righteousness. (Jer. 33:15–16)

These passages prophesy that in the days of the messianic Kingdom, God will raise up a descendant of David—a "righteous Branch" or "Branch of Righteousness"—who will bring about redemption. He will be called "ADONAI our Righteousness." What's amazing is *Adonai Tsidkenu* ("the

Lord our Righteousness") and *Tzemah Tsadik* ("the Righteous Branch")
are two of the primary titles of the Messiah in both biblical and rabbinic
thought. The rabbis say this in the *Midrash*:

> "What is the name of the Messiah King?" Rabbi Abba Bar-Kahana
> said: "The Lord is his name that they will call him: The Lord, Our
> Righteousness."[7]

Rabbi Yehoshua ben Levi pointed out, "His name is Tzemah—as it is
stated: 'Behold a man, Tzemah is his name, and he will sprout [*yitzmah*]'
(Zechariah 6:12)."[8] He will sprout like a branch.

Yeshua healing "the blind man" (276) demonstrated that He is the
"Lord our Righteousness" (276), who is the promised messianic Righteous
Branch (*Tzemah Tzadik*), the Redeemer of Israel.

There are other significant words in Scripture that have the numerical
value of 276. John 1:14 says, "And the Word became flesh and tabernacled
among us. We looked upon His glory, the glory of the one and only from
the Father, full of grace and truth." The Hebrew word translated "looked
upon" also has a numerical value of 276! There is powerful symbolism
here. We have blind eyes, yet we must look—to see—with our eyes.

## The Secret of Yeshua's Saliva

Yeshua spat in the dirt and made mud with His saliva. He placed the
clump on the eyes of the blind man and told him to wash in the Pool
of Siloam. This seems like a strange way to heal someone. Could there
be more to the story than in all the other miracles of Yeshua? Let's
find out.

When the man rinsed his eyes, he saw for the first time in his life. To fully comprehend the magnitude of this miracle and its deeper message, we need to consider the actions Yeshua took. The most important part of this miracle was using saliva to make the mud. This man was born blind, which means he had a genetic defect. Therefore, he needed to experience spiritual, physical, and genetic healing.

If you've ever watched crime shows, you're familiar with detectives trying to trick their suspects into drinking something so they can take the cup. Why? Because saliva contains DNA. Yeshua was transferring His divine DNA via His saliva to this man who was born blind because of an inherited genetic defect. Like He had created Adam from the dirt, Yeshua performed this miracle with mud and saliva because it was a new-creation miracle. By putting the mud onto the man's eyes, Yeshua was essentially saying, "Look, I'm creating your eyes anew, just like in the very beginning when We created man in Our image. I am doing a work of new creation in you." Yeshua has the power to heal us genetically, even from disabilities we are born with!

## The Significance of Saliva for Ancient Jews

From a Jewish perspective, this story has something deeper at play. Yeshua's use of saliva communicated an important message about His origin, His paternity, and His role as God's firstborn Son and heir to the Kingdom of God—the true descendant of David and the promised Messiah.

Biblically, being the firstborn is significant. The firstborn was entitled to a double portion of everything his father owned. Historically, the right to inherit the firstborn's double portion could be contested. To win, the one claiming to be the firstborn had to prove he was the firstborn of his mother and not just his father. This principle gets complicated if the woman had been previously married, the father had multiple wives, or the child was illegitimate. There was a belief among some rabbis in the first century that the saliva of the firstborn had medicinal and healing properties. They believed that families could use the spit of the firstborn to prove that a son was indeed the firstborn and had the right to receive the firstborn's blessing. In the Talmud, there's an example of this in which a son demonstrated that he genuinely was the firstborn by putting some of his saliva on a man's ailing eyes, which healed the man's eyes. The Talmud states, "The spittle of the firstborn of a father is healing, but that of the firstborn of the mother is not healing."[9]

Yeshua's enemies accused Him of being an illegitimate son, but Yeshua's teaching implied He did not have a human father but a heavenly Father. He is the Chosen One who comes from and was sent by the Father. The miraculous healing of the man born blind should have proven Yeshua's claim. Only the saliva of the Father's firstborn Son could supernaturally heal a man who had been born blind. Amazing! God reveals Himself in the details.

Paraphrasing John 8:16–19, Yeshua said, "Look, I'm the One sent by the Father in heaven." And they responded in confusion, asking, "Who's Your father?" They didn't get it. Then He performed this miracle with saliva to prove that He was the firstborn whom God sent. Yeshua demonstrated in this miracle that He is who He says He is—His divine origins, His true identity as the Messiah, God, the Word made flesh. But unfortunately, many of the Judean leaders rejected the sign. Although the one born blind could see who Yeshua was, those who claimed to have deep spiritual sight and insight remained spiritually blind. That's the irony in this story. Yeshua is the Great Physician, and every one of us needs to have our eyes healed. Faith is about sight.

## Eyes of Faith

The author of Hebrews stated, "Now faith is the substance of things hoped for, the evidence of realities not seen" (11:1). All of us need our eyes opened. Too often, we fail to see the fullness of who God is, His promises, and what He's doing in our lives. We grumble and complain like the Children of Israel did in the wilderness, even after experiencing miracle after miracle and being fed supernatural bread from heaven. The religious leaders in Yeshua's day watched Him perform miracles, yet they did not believe He was Messiah. Instead, they were angry at Him because He healed the blind man on the *Shabbat*—the Sabbath. As they had done when Yeshua healed the paralytic at the pool of Bethesda, they believed Yeshua violated the Sabbath, but He didn't. They were the genuinely blind ones. Healing this man's eyes brought Yeshua's divine identity into the light. This miracle pricked the religious Pharisees' pride, but it revealed the Lord's overwhelming mercy and kindness. It showed that nothing is impossible with Him, even genetic and congenital diseases, and that every person, even broken societal outcasts, are important. He truly is the Great Physician of body and soul.

Unless God opens our eyes by His grace, we remain blind in unbelief. There are different levels of unbelief in our hearts. Perhaps we believe in Yeshua as our Savior, as our Messiah, but we don't have the faith to believe that He will show up in certain circumstances of our lives. All of us have places where we struggle with fear and with faith. Even the disciples weren't immune to unbelief. God wants to give all of us greater ability to see—greater faith. The opening of the eyes of the blind man is a new creation miracle that elicits a response. We respond either in faith, or unbelief, as the Pharisees did. Faith is about having the sight to see beyond our limitations and our circumstances and to trust God. When responded to in faith, one touch from Yeshua can open your eyes and change everything.

## The Significance of the Place

After spreading mud made with saliva on the blind man's eyes, Yeshua told him to go wash in the Pool of Siloam. In Hebrew, "Siloam" is *shiloach*, which means "sent one." The Pool of Siloam is also known as the King's Pool because kings were anointed there. It was likely a place where the poor would bathe. The pilgrims of Jerusalem would go to do *mikvah*—to ritually purify themselves in the water so they could ascend to the Temple in a state of ritual purity. Before entering the Temple, they had to immerse themselves in the water to wash their past away.

The blind man went into the water with the mud on his eyes; he washed his eyes, and Yeshua healed them. What Yeshua did by immersing the blind man in the water followed the Torah. But it also demonstrated the man's spiritual cleansing of his shame, hurt, and guilt. It was all washed away by the healing power of Yeshua. He was being made into a new creation. This miracle occurred at the Pool of the Sent One because Yeshua is the One sent from the Father and is the King of Israel.

## "I Am the Light of the World"

Light is an important aspect of our lives. We need it when the sun goes down to illuminate our homes. If our power goes out, we must find a flashlight or a candle to help us not bump into furniture. We can't drive at night without headlights. Outside, we have the sun by day and the moon by night. So, yes, light is important to all of us.

In John 8:12 Yeshua said, "I am the light of the world," or *ani ohr Haolam* in Hebrew.

This Hebrew phrase numerically is 419. Why is that interesting? Because the phrase "I am Messiah (*Mashiach*)" also equals 419. Yeshua was pointing to Himself. But there's more about the number 419:

- The phrase "righteous leader of the generation (*tzadik dor*)" equals 419. In Jewish thought and tradition, Messiah must be the *tzadik dor*. In rabbinic Judaism, a rabbi is more than a teacher. He is someone who cleaves to God and hears God's voice. And God uses him and speaks to him in a very special way. He is the leader of leaders.
- The word *Datyah*, or "law of the Lord," equals 419 from the Hebrew letters (*dalet*/[4] + *tav*/[400] + *yud*/[10] + *hei*/[5] = 419).
- The Hebrew words for "the source of wisdom," *mah-kohr chokmah*, equal 419.
- In Greek, the phrase "to teach" is *didactoi*. John 6:45 says, "It is written in the Prophets, 'They will all be *taught* by God.' Everyone who has listened and learned from the Father comes to Me" (emphasis mine).
- Another Greek word, *exaireō*, equals 419. It means "to deliver" as in Galatians 1:4, "that he could deliver us" (NKJV).
- "They shall enter," as in the Promised Land, *tavi'u* in Hebrew (Deut. 12:10–12), equals 419.

When Yeshua healed the man born blind, He said, "I am the Light of the World [419]." He was declaring, "I am the Messiah [419]," "the Righteous Leader of the Generation [419]," who is the "source of wisdom

[419]" who "taught [419]" "the law of the LORD [419]" and was the One who fulfilled it "so that He could deliver us [419]" who believe so that "they can enter [419]" the ultimate Promised Land—the messianic Kingdom![10]

## A Shocking Statement

This statement—"I am the light of the world"—shocked the religious leaders, and understanding the context will tell you why. Yeshua uttered those words about Himself in the context of *Sukkot*, the biblical holiday known as the Feast of Tabernacles. Jewish people associate *Sukkot* with God's glorious light. *Sukkot* celebrates God's presence, protection, and provision for the *b'nei* (Children) of *Yisra'el* (Israel) during their forty years of wilderness wanderings. *Sukkot* is the third biblical holiday of the fall season. Every year for this festival, my family and I build what is known as a *sukkah*. This temporary structure reminds us of the nonpermanent booths our ancestors dwelled in during their time in the wilderness. The *sukkah* is a booth that must have at least three enclosed sides. It must be a temporary structure; you eat in it for seven days. Frequently, you sleep in it. *Sukkot* helps us remember what happened during the time of the wilderness.

According to the Jewish perspective, the rabbis tell us the booths point to the clouds of glory because God formed a tabernacle, a *sukkah*, over the people.[11] The clouds of glory covered them on top, bottom, and the two sides (north, south, east, and west). They covered them to protect them from the heat of the day, the cold at night, the scorpions, and other elements. Divine protection formed a *sukkah* over them. According to tradition, these clouds of glory radiated the supernatural light of the Lord. The same light shone on the first day of Creation. *Sukkah* that we dwell in today connects light to the glory of God.

*Sukkot* was, and is, the most joyous of all the Jewish holidays. It is known as "the time for our rejoicing," or *zeman simchateinu* in Hebrew. In the Temple in Jerusalem, four golden lamps were used only on *Sukkot*. They were placed in the courtyard of the women. Each one of these candelabras contained four bowls. They were fifty cubits high, or seventy-five feet tall. These lampstands towered over the walls of the Temple. The Talmud tells us that priests lit these lamps, and their light would illuminate all four corners of Jerusalem.[12] This extraordinary light reminded the Jewish people of the clouds of glory and the pillar of fire, which was the light of all lights or the *Schechinah* (sheh-KHEE-nah) glory—the manifest presence of the Lord that filled the first Tabernacle in the wilderness and Solomon's Temple (1 Kings 8:10–11).

When Yeshua said, "I am the light of the world," this light is what He meant. He was saying, "The glory that was with your ancestors in the wilderness, the glory that led your ancestors by a cloud of glory by day and a pillar of fire by night—that was Me! The glory that covered your ancestors, protected and provided for them, *that was Me! I am the fulfillment of that!*" Yeshua told them and is telling us, "If you believe in Me, I will be your covering and light!" Just as Israel dwelled in the tabernacles, we must be in Yeshua's light. We must be under His clouds of protection, completely immersed and surrounded by Him.

The light associated with *Sukkot* is the supernatural light of God's glorious presence. This supernatural light is the light of life and healing and is ultimately found in the person of Yeshua as John stated: "In Him was life, and the life was the light of men. . . . The true light, coming into the world, gives light to every man. . . . And the Word became flesh and tabernacled among us. We looked upon His glory, the glory of the one and only" (John 1:4, 9, 14). The light of God's glorious Presence, which gives life and tabernacled in the Tabernacle, most fully dwells in the person of Yeshua-Jesus and is the route of healing and wholeness—in the same way the sun helps create life on earth and its light dispels darkness, allowing us to see. Yeshua's light transformed the darkness of the blind man into sight and allowed him to experience the true joy and meaning of *Sukkot*.

## Seeing the Light

When God created Adam and Eve and put them in the Garden, He walked with them, and His glory was a daily occurrence. They were not blind to it. People often picture Eden as a tabernacle, in which God came and fellowshipped with Adam in the cool of the day. Then Adam and Eve sinned, and God expelled them from Eden. Because of sin, a separation between God and us and His glory occurred. The Lord no longer walked with humanity.

Over time, as sin spread, that disconnection became wider, and we lost physical closeness with God. We also lost the Divine Light. The light of the first three days of Creation was not the sun's light. God created that light on the fourth day. The light that existed on the first three days of Creation was purely spiritual light. It was the Divine Light of God that Adam and Eve enjoyed. In Jewish and rabbinic thought, garments of light clothed man. That's why God opened their eyes after they ate from the Tree of Knowledge of Good and Evil. They were ashamed and felt naked because, initially, God's glory covered them. Before the Fall, they had garments of light that radiated God's glory. After the Fall, they lost the light of God's presence and no longer radiated the glory. Think about Moses on the mountain. In God's presence, he shone with the glory of God and had to put a veil over his head because it scared the people. Moses was in

God's presence for only forty days, several centuries after the Fall. Can you imagine the light that Adam and Eve radiated when covered by God's light? And the reality is that when we spend time in God's presence like Moses did, a light radiates from us.

I'll never forget when I was little how I loved these glow-in-the-dark shoelaces. When I'd leave my shoes out in the sun all day, at night, they would glow. I walked in the light. I also had a toy shield that would glow in the dark if you left it out in the light. Friends, if you stay in the light, you will glow in the night. As we abide in Yeshua and spend time in His presence, the Lord's light shines and radiates in and through us.

Interestingly, there's only one letter difference between the Hebrew words for light and skins. Skins (*ohr*) begins with the letter *ayin* (ע) and light (*ohr*) begins with the letter *aleph* (א). That one letter makes all the difference.

In Hebrew, every number has both a positive and negative aspect. The letter *ayin* has the numerical value of 70 and means "eye." Both 70 and the eye connect to exile in the negative. The eye led Adam and Eve to sin in the Garden. This is the root of all exiles. Due to the sin of the Tower of Babel, God confused the languages of the people. According to Jewish tradition, the Lord confused their language (Gen. 11:7) by dividing them into seventy different nations and dialects.[13] *Babel*, in Hebrew, means Babylon. Israel was exiled to Babylon (the same place as the famous Tower of Babel) for seventy years. Israel went into Babylonian exile in the days of Daniel and Jeremiah for seventy years. The Second Temple was destroyed in AD 70, which began the Jewish people's longest exile from Jerusalem and, ultimately, the land of Israel. *Aleph* is a letter that represents God, as most of the divine names of God (*Elohim*, for example) begin with the letter *aleph*. *Light* begins with the letter *aleph*. There's one letter difference between *exile* and *redemption*. The Lord wants to transform our *ayin* into an *aleph*. He wants to transform our exile into redemption, our darkness into light, and our blindness into sight.

## From *Aleph* to *Ayin*

Moses said to God on the mountain, "Please, show me Your glory!" (Ex. 33:18). That's what we should be asking for too. And God wants to answer. He wants to restore our vision so we're not blinded but can see in the spiritual world and discern the difference between light and darkness.

## Finding the Hidden Light

When Adam and Eve sinned, God hid the divine light, but not completely. He hid it under His throne for the righteous in the world to come in the messianic Kingdom. He also allows us to get a glimpse of the light. But how can we experience that divine light? By opening His Word. God hid the light in the Scriptures. Proverbs 6:23 tells us, "*For the* mitzvah *[commandments] is a lamp,* Torah *a light,* and corrective discipline the way of life" (emphasis mine). When we delve deep into God's Word, meditate on it deeply, and engage with it, we have His light. When we don't stay on the surface but genuinely seek and study His Word, it illuminates our lives and gives us revelation and wisdom.

The Hebrew word for light occurs five times on the first day of Creation (Gen. 1:3–5). I believe this alludes to the five books of the Torah, which is the foundational source of illumination for Israel. The New Testament disciples studied these five books. God's light is revealed and released when we study the Word, both Old and New Testaments.

God also hid the light, even more, in the person of Messiah. Jewish tradition makes this connection between Messiah and the divine light. What special divine light are the Jewish people yearning for? The light of the Messiah, as it was written: "God saw that the light was good. So God distinguished the light from the darkness" (Gen. 1:4). This teaches us that God foresaw Messiah and His activities before the creation of the world.[14] Fourth-century Jewish Talmudist Rabba said, "And the light dwells with Him" alludes to the royal Messiah.[15]

## Light and the New Covenant

The New Covenant (New Testament) stands in agreement with these texts and elaborates even further:

In Him was life, and the life was the light of men. And the light shines in the darkness, and the darkness did not comprehend it. . . . That was the true Light which gives light to every man coming into the world. (John 1:4–5, 7 NKJV)

Yeshua spoke to them again, saying, "I am the light of the world. The one who follows Me will no longer walk in darkness, but will have the light of life." (John 8:12)

But I saw no temple in it [great city], for the Lord God Almighty and the Lamb are its temple. The city had no need of the sun or of the moon to shine in it, for the glory of God illuminated it. The Lamb is its light. And the nations of those who are saved shall walk in its light, and the kings of the earth bring their glory and honor into it. Its gates shall not be shut at all by day (there shall be no night there). And they shall bring the glory and the honor of the nations into it. (Rev. 21:22–26, emphasis mine)

Based on these passages, we must conclude that Messiah is the source of this unique light and the One who will cause the lost light of the first three days of Creation to shine again in the messianic age. When that time occurs, all the redeemed ones will bask in His divine light and find healing and blessing.

As Rabbi Paul wrote, "For God, who said, 'Let light shine out of darkness,' is the One who has shone in our hearts, to give the light of the knowledge of the glory of God in the face of Messiah" (2 Cor. 4:6). This miracle reminds us that Yeshua is the light of the world!

## Restored at Sukkot

At the end of days, the Divine Light will be restored at *Sukkot*, the Feast of Tabernacles, when it all ties together. Yeshua made the "light of the world" statement in the context of *Sukkot*, connected to the Divine Light and its restoration, and to the Kingdom. *Sukkot* is the Kingdom holiday. It's a seventh holiday that lasts for seven days and in the seventh month (*Tishrei*). Zechariah 14:6–9 tells us,

In that day there will be no light, cold or frost. It will be a day known only to ADONAI, neither day nor night—even in the evening time there will be light. Moreover, in that day living waters will flow from Jerusalem, half toward the eastern sea and half toward the western sea, both in the summer and in the winter. ADONAI will then be King over all the earth. In that day ADONAI will be *Echad* [One] and His Name *Echad*.

Zechariah prophesied that we will celebrate *Sukkot* in the end of days: "Then all the survivors from all the nations that attacked Jerusalem will go up from year to year to worship the King, ADONAI-Tzva'ot, and to celebrate *Sukkot*" (14:16). On *Sukkot*, Yeshua called Himself two things: the light of the world and the living water (John 4:10; 7:38). The light that Zechariah promised in the messianic Kingdom, you can experience today, and in it find life and blessing, revelation, illumination, and transformation. But the other promise was the living waters that would flow from Jerusalem (Zech. 14:8). Those living waters will turn the Dead Sea into life!

## I Was Blind but Now I See

I travel a lot, even taking groups of people to Israel. Sometimes when I wake up in the middle of the night, the room is completely dark. I can't find my way to the bathroom. I bump into things and need to turn on the light so I can see. As we've studied, God "turned on the light" at Creation and He turned on the light for this blind man who could now see. *Sukkot* is connected to light. The lamps lit Jerusalem not only with the *Shechinah*, the divine presence of God that was with Israel in the wilderness, but also the Messiah. The light pointed to *Ha'or Gadol* (the Great Light). The Messiah brings the light of life to the living and the dead, this blind man, and to you and me.

Darkness represents death, but light represents life. This blind man found a new life. Yeshua came that you might have life and have it more abundantly (John 10:10). The first thing God did was call forth the light out of the darkness. The light dispelled the darkness, chaos, and void. When we receive Yeshua as our light, we can command the darkness to go, and we can abide in the light of Yeshua and in the light of His Word. When we do, the darkness and chaos cannot ultimately remain. When we invite Him into our lives, it's not merely the prayer of salvation but an opening up to the light of His Word, His presence, and His love that fills that void where there was once darkness.

Darkness also connects to sadness. *Sukkot* is a time of great rejoicing and joy. The joy we have in Yeshua can transform our sadness into gladness. Before Yeshua healed the blind man in John 9, He said that the man's blindness would reveal the works of God. The Lord did not cause this man's blindness and pain, but He used it for a greater purpose. There was something redemptive and meaningful about it. God has a way of bringing purpose to our pain and hardship. Remember, God works all for good (Rom. 8:28). He wants to bring meaning out of the significant hurts you've experienced. Paul wrote, "For our trouble, light and momentary, is producing for us an eternal weight of glory far beyond all comparison, as we look not at what can be seen but at what cannot be seen. For what can be seen is temporary, but what cannot be seen is eternal" (2 Cor. 4:17–18). Though we can't always see it, our momentary troubles produce something eternal and glorious in us. It's the glory of God's presence shining on and through us, filling the void far beyond all comparison to anything this world has to offer. Yes, the struggle is real, but it will be worth it in the end because we will be living in His light.

The miracle of the blind man shows that your loss and pain are not pointless but contain a promise that God can redeem them and use them for the greater good and to reveal His glory. Yeshua can transform your *Oy* into joy! Your pain is not meaningless—God can use it for good! Let His light shine into your life, bringing joy and healing and declaring His glory.

# NINE

# THE SIGNS AND SECRETS
# OF THE NETS

In this chapter, we will look at one of my favorite miracles—the miracle of the nets that don't break, or what some people refer to as the miracle of the full nets—found in John 21. The story illustrates God's provision, yet it also teaches us so much more, as we'll discover in the next few pages.

It was a challenging time. Peter had denied the Lord, but then Yeshua rose on the third day. Peter and a few disciples decided to go fishing in the Sea of Galilee. They had fished all night and caught nothing! Then, the miracle occurred. Yeshua was on the beach, but they didn't recognize Him. He called to them and instructed them to cast their nets again. They obeyed and this time their nets were filled to the point of almost breaking (John 21:1–6).

I believe this is incredibly meaningful. The disciples' nets were almost to the point of breaking, representing the abundant and expanding catch. I believe that there is a great catch coming for you as well, and God wants to fill and expand your "nets" abundantly.

## Faith, Not Fear

Think about it for a moment. Peter had denied the Lord. He probably thought there was no longer a major role for him and certainly not as the leader or rock of this new Yeshua-Jesus movement. He returned to a place of familiarity. Maybe you've heard this old saying: When the going gets tough, the tough go fishing.

The Hebrew word for fish is *dag* (or sometimes spelled *daag*) and it is a clue to finding a deeper meaning. *Dag* also means "anxiety." For example, Psalm 38:18 says, "For I confess my iniquity; I am full of *anxiety* [*dag*] because of my sin" (NASB, emphasis mine). The Hebrew word for fish can also mean "to be anxious, concerned, or to fear."

Peter and the disciples were fishing from a place of anxiety and worry about their future. God doesn't want you to be anxious or worried about what may or may not happen to you. Peter had anxiety and fear, but we must understand that fear is false faith. True faith believes the best, while fear thinks the worst. Fear undermines faith and corrupts our vision. It causes us to believe in the worst possible future. Fear leads to pessimism and cynicism, causing us to run around like Chicken Little, believing that the sky is falling when it isn't. Fear brings cursing, but faith brings blessing. Fear imprisons and paralyzes, while faith empowers. Faith propels and gives us momentum. Faith helps us to overcome. First John 5:4–5 says, "Everyone born of God overcomes the world. This is the victory that has overcome the world, even our faith. Who is it that overcomes the world? Only the one who believes that Jesus is the Son of God" (NIV). The Greek verb for "overcomes" is *nikaō*. It means "to conquer, prevail."[1] Yeshua came for us to have victory and conquer the fears that can drag us down or cause us to make poor decisions.

Bottom line, if you want your nets to be full, you must operate out of a place of faith, not fear, worry, and anxiety. When you stay in fear, your net is always going to be empty. When you live in faith, the miraculous comes into your life, and your net becomes full.

## Operating in the Power of the Holy Spirit

The only way for your net to get full of divine favor and blessings is by operating in the power of the *Ruach*, the power of the Spirit. Often in the book of John, words can have a double meaning. I believe that's true in this story because Scripture says that the disciples were fishing at night. They were fishing in the dark. While it's normal for a fisherman to fish at night in the dark, we find, especially in the book of John, a play of imagery between light and darkness and night and day. Night can represent operating without the light of God's presence in our lives. In a sense, the disciples were operating in their own strength and according to their own plan. Again, I think Peter returned to his former profession because he didn't know what to do with his life. He thought he might as well pick up where he left off. But that's a going-back-to-Egypt attitude.

The catch of fish came with the sunrise through the direction of the Son, Yeshua. When He told them to cast the nets again, they listened and were empowered. We need to operate in the *Ruach* to see the abundance in our lives. Sometimes we've caught nothing, or we're experiencing lack, because we're not operating according to God's plan, wisdom, and power. We need our nets strengthened by continually relying on the power of the Spirit. Here's what may help you—take time to pray and ask the Holy Spirit to guide you in all aspects of your life. I guarantee your nets will be strengthened.

Often, we come up with great ideas for our next move in life. We ask God to bless our ideas without asking God what His plans or intentions are for our lives. It's not *great* ideas that we need but *God* ideas implemented in the power of the Spirit that will help us experience the great catch. This is the point of John 15:5: "I am the vine and you are the branches. Those who stay *united* with me, and I with them, are the ones who bear much fruit; because apart from me *you can't do a thing*" (CJB, emphasis mine). In Greek, do you know what the word *thing* means? It means "nothing." In Hebrew, *efes* means "nothing, zilch, zero." And in Yiddish, such a colorful language, the phrase is *gornisht mit gornisht*, which means, "A whole lot of nothing."

It is not by our power or might but by God's Spirit that nets become abundantly full.

I know a successful businessman who owned a large retail clothing store. He's a billionaire who came from Asia to the United States. He barely received a high school education and worked at full-service gas stations pumping gas, checking oil, and cleaning windshields for years. He would often ask the people whom he was helping, "What do you do for work?" Soon, he realized that many of the most successful people who drove the nicest cars were in the clothing and fashion business. So, he and his wife saved enough money to buy a failing store, turned it around, and created a clothing empire. He also gave significantly to Kingdom causes. When I asked him how he built such a big business and how it became such a huge success, he said that his success was simple. He told me, "I'm not that educated. I don't have an MBA. What I do is sit with God for hours each day and I lay all the opportunities and decisions before Him and pray. Then, I wait for God to answer." *Wow*. I mean, talk about a business strategy!

I was blown away by that thought. He was a successful entrepreneur and businessman. He didn't have a college education. I don't know how far he went in high school. Yet he was so well-off. Why? Because he operated in the power of the Spirit, according to the plan of God, laying it all before Him in prayer. If our nets are going to be full, we must operate in the power, direction, and leadership of the Holy Spirit.

Interestingly, the disciples could have ignored the man on the beach and never lifted a finger. They didn't recognize it was Yeshua and could have not listened to the advice—they were experienced fishermen, after all. But they did listen. I believe the Spirit prompted them to cast their nets a different way, and they followed the leading of the Spirit. They listened to that inner voice of God, and when they did, there was a great catch, and then Yeshua revealed Himself.

## The Secret of Operating in the Power of God's Word

For your nets to be full, you must strengthen them with God's Word—both the Old and the New Testaments. Yeshua said, "Cast your nets again on the right side of the boat" (v. 6). Why? Because the right side, in Jewish thought, is the side associated with the Torah, the Five Books of Moses, the foundation of the Hebrew Scriptures, and God's covenant with Israel and the Jewish people.

There is a part of the Saturday *Shabbat* morning prayer service when you take the handwritten sacred Torah out of its ark (the ornamental chamber or shaft in the synagogue for storage) and you process it around the congregation. When you hold the Torah, you always carry it on the right side. And when you unroll it, you always do it beginning from the right side. The right side in the Bible and Jewish thought is the side of the Word; it is the side of the Torah.

It is also the side of water. Water and Torah are associated. We read

Torah three days a week in the synagogue. Why? Because you can't live more than three days without water. As I mentioned earlier, just as we can't live physically without the water for our bodies, our souls can't live more than three days without the "water" of the Torah. Jewish people read the Torah Monday, Thursdays, and Saturdays to make sure we never go more than three days without Scripture.

There's another connection between water and the Word. Isaiah 11:9 says, "They will not hurt or destroy in all My holy mountain, for the earth will be full of the knowledge of ADONAI, as the waters cover the sea." In this chapter, Isaiah was speaking about a great revival, a move of God, and the establishment of the Kingdom. He's connecting the water and the Word, which connects to the right side.

## The Secret of 153 Fish

When the disciples brought in the great catch of fish, there were 153 fish in the net. There is a deep implication in the number 153 and how it connects to what we've discussed. Jewish people today read through the Five Books of Moses over a one-year period. Part of the fun celebration of *Sukkot* is when, on the last day, we finish reading the Torah (*Simchat Torah*). We finish Deuteronomy and then begin in Genesis 1:1 again. Jewish scholars and rabbis recognize that in first-century Israel, it wasn't read over one year. Most Jewish communities in the land of Israel were on a triennial cycle (every three years), so every three or more years (probably three and a half years), the first-century Jews finished the entire reading of the Torah. According to Jerusalem Talmud, triennial reading was often broken into 153 readings.[2]

The twelve disciples, along with other men and women who followed Yeshua, were not the most elite scholars of their day. Peter and John were fishermen. How could they amaze the religious elite? Acts 4:13 says, "Now when they saw the boldness of Peter and John and figured out they *were laymen without training*, they were *amazed*. They began to realize that these men *had been with Yeshua*" (emphasis mine). Here's something else—how long did Yeshua's ministry last? Three and a half years. His ministry lasted three and a half years; the Torah portions were read over three and a half years (153 readings). Yeshua, over the three and a half years, walked with His disciples on this earth and taught His followers every portion of the Torah. Then, He gave them the best understanding and the deepest insights into the true meaning of the Torah and the prophets. This is how His disciples became so knowledgeable that they could preach with such insight and authority that even the religious leaders were astounded. In the same way Yeshua trained His disciples, He calls each of us to delve into the depth of Scripture, both Old and New, so that we might also become scribes for the Kingdom (Matt. 13:52).

As followers of Yeshua, we are called to this. Who wants half an inheritance? The full inheritance is Old and New. If we want our nets to be full, and we want to fish from the place of the Scriptures, we need to study both the Old Testament and New Testament. Hebrews 4:12 calls Scripture a double-edged sword. Why? One thought is that its double edges are the Old and New, and both sides need to be sharp.

Continuing to dig, we find there's still more to the number 153 and the Torah. There are two ways to spell *fish*. One way to spell *fish*, *dag*, is the with the letters *dalet* (4) and *gimmel* (3), which equals 7. The Hebrew word for fish has a numerical value of 7. We celebrate the Torah on *Shavuot*. *Shavuot* (Pentecost) means "weeks." God gave the Torah seven weeks (or forty-nine days) from Passover. When we read the Torah on Saturdays (*Shabbat*), it's broken up into seven readings. Most of *Shavuot* (Pentecost) connects to the number 7—seven days a week, seven weeks until God gave the Torah, and seven readings of the Torah on *Shabbat*. Seven is the number of fullness and completion. God's Word brings His fullness and completion. His Word connects to the number 7 and the number of fish the disciples caught. The number 153 represents an understanding of the Torah, from Genesis to Deuteronomy.

# Yeshua's Identity

Isaiah 41:13 says, "For I hold you by your right hand—I, the LORD your God. And I say to you, 'Don't be afraid. I am here to help you'" (NLT). The phrase "I am the Lord" (*ani Elohim*) equals 153.

Yeshua told the disciples exactly when and where to cast the net to bring in the great catch! Like turning the water into wine, this miracle demonstrated Messiah Yeshua's divine omniscience, omnipotence, and power over creation. It also shows us that He teaches us what is good and leads us exactly to what He's called us to do. We don't need to fear; God is near and wants to help.

## The Promised Messianic King

The number 153 also points to Yeshua as the divine messianic King. Psalm 24:8 says, "Who is this King of glory? *ADONAI* strong and mighty, *ADONAI* mighty in battle!" The phrase "King of glory" has a numerical value of 153. Yeshua, the promised messianic King, is one of the central themes of the book of John. John 1:41 says, "First he finds his own brother Simon and tells him, 'We've found the Messiah!' (which is translated Anointed One)." John wrote about the Messiah who descended from King David.

We've been studying the miracles and mysteries found in the book of John. The reason for these signs and wonders was to demonstrate that He, Yeshua, was and is the promised messianic King. We find this throughout the book of John and, if you'll remember, at the very end, in John 20: 30–31,

> *Yeshua* performed many other signs in the presence of the disciples, which are not written in this book. But these things have been written so that you may believe that *Yeshua is Mashiach Ben-Elohim [Messiah Son of God]*, and that by believing you may have life in His name.

From beginning to end, John tried to show Yeshua as the promised messianic King of Israel, and the number 153 supports that. Because who is the King of glory? It is Yeshua—153.

You'll remember from our discussion of bread that from a Hebraic perspective, the king was to be the provider and sustainer of his people. When the kings of Israel obeyed God, God provided the early and the latter rain, which produced abundant crops. God blessed.

The great catch of fish shows that Yeshua was the promised messianic King who provided for His people. He also provides for us when we obey His specific directions and then give Him the glory for our catch.

There's so much more we could cover concerning Yeshua and the number 153. The phrase "the Passover Lamb" in Hebrew equals 153. He is the fulfillment of Passover and our redemption. In the account of the crucifixion, "His clothes were divided" and "rolled in" (in Greek) also equal 153. He died as the Passover Lamb, His clothes were divided during His crucifixion, and Joseph of Arimathea rolled the stone in front of the tomb. Yeshua's death, burial, and resurrection connect to the number of fish—153. That's amazing!

# The Catch Is Coming

I'm convinced that spiritually and prophetically, we live in a John 21 moment. Part of this moment is that a great catch of souls is coming. It's time to restore the inheritance of the Torah and the Jewish roots to the nations and the Jewish people who are lost. It's time for the church to wake up. There is an awakening going on today. Christians need to understand the Jewishness of the Bible, Yeshua, and their Hebrew roots. And at the same time, so many Jewish people are secular and don't even know what it means to be Jewish. They may have a Jewish parent and some cultural traditions, but they need to come back to their roots as well. It must happen through Yeshua, though. Yeshua is the way, the truth, and the life. No one comes to the Father except through Him (John 14:6).

What can bring both groups back? It's understanding the Hebrew Scriptures and the Torah concerning and connecting Yeshua and His teachings. He is the fulfillment and the One who brings the fullness. This is a key piece of the net that the body—the people of Messiah—desperately needs. We often pray, "Your kingdom come, Your will be done on earth as it is in heaven." That's not some wishy-washy prayer. Whatever the Kingdom looks like, that's how we need to live our lives. So what is Torah's role in the Kingdom? Micah 4:1–3 says,

> But at the end of days the mountain of ADONAI's House will be established as chief of the mountains, and will be raised above the hills. Peoples will flow up to it. Then many nations will go and say: "Come, let us go up to the mountain of ADONAI, to the House of the God of Jacob! Then He will direct us in His ways, and we will walk in His paths." For Torah will go forth from Zion, and the word of ADONAI from Jerusalem.

He will judge between many peoples and decide for mighty nations far off. They will beat their swords into plowshares, and their spears into pruning shears. Nation will not lift up sword against nation, nor will they learn war again.

If the Torah is fundamental in the Kingdom and central to the proclamation of what Yeshua is doing from Zion, shouldn't we seek to understand it? The Torah is going to be foundational in how He judges people and nations. There is wisdom and revelation in Scripture's principles. I'm not saying that all Gentiles have to keep the letter of the commandments of the Jewish people. We are saved by grace through faith, not the works of the Law (Rom. 3:28; Eph. 2:8–9). Yet there is a foundation to the New Testament that you can't truly get without an understanding of the Old Testament.

It's not solely about the future. Luke wrote in Acts 21:20, "And when they heard, they began glorifying God. They said, 'You see, brother, how many myriads there are among the Jewish people who have believed— and they are all zealous for the Torah.'" There were thousands of Jewish people who believed, and they did not throw out the Torah. A Greco-Roman anti-Jewish worldview was foreign to the New Testament, because Luke wrote that the Jewish believers were all zealous for the Torah. If the first followers of Yeshua were zealous for the Torah and passionate about learning and understanding how it applied to their lives, shouldn't we be as well? We should be as passionate and zealous for the Torah as the disciples of Yeshua were. After all, everything in the Torah, as well as the entire Bible, points to Yeshua. From the first letter of the Bible in Genesis 1:1—the Hebrew letter B or beit, meaning bereisheet, or "beginning"—to the last word of the book of Revelation—"Amen"—it's all significant. The last letter of Scripture is the letter nun (נ). As I mentioned earlier, the first and last letters of the Bible in Hebrew spell Ben. **Be**N in Hebrew means *son*—from beginning to end, the Bible points to the Son and finds its fulfillment in the Son. To pull in a full catch of wisdom, we need our nets strengthened by the Torah and all of God's Word.

## Four Principles for Keeping Your Nets Full

God wants to give you nets (abundance, provision, wisdom, etc.) that don't break and are full of His blessings. But to see fullness come and find full nets in your life,

- you must operate out of faith, not fear.
- you must operate out of the power and direction of the Holy Spirit—not in your strength, your wisdom, or according to your own will—asking God to bless what you do.
- you must find what God is blessing, and wants to bless, and participate in it.
- you must also operate in love and relational unity.

The Holy Spirit flows like a river. The easiest way to operate in fullness is to find out where He is going, jump in, and go with the flow! When we are moving in the current or power of the Holy Spirit and not our strength, we can do amazing things. The disciples had fished all night in their strength and wisdom and caught nothing, but when Yeshua spoke, they had to follow His lead. The result? Nearly bursting nets.

We must operate from deep wisdom and understanding of God's Word—again, both Old and New, which is the Hebrew Bible and the Torah (the foundation). That is the promise of the Scriptures. God told

Joshua, "This book of the *Torah* should not depart from your mouth—you are to meditate on it day and night, so that you may be careful to do everything written in it. For then you will make your ways prosperous and then you will be successful" (Josh. 1:8). God gave us an instruction manual packed full of not only instructions but promises. We read something similar in Psalm 1:2–3:

> But his delight is in the Torah of *Adonai*, and on His *Torah* he meditates day and night. He will be like a planted tree over streams of water, producing its fruit during its season. Its leaf never droops—but in all he does, he succeeds.

Friends, do you want to prosper? Succeed? Do you want all the fullness God can bring to your nets? These are four foundational practices we must learn and embrace.

## Fishing from the Left

John 21:6 says, "He said to them, 'Throw the net off the right side of the boat, and you'll find some.' So they threw the net, and they were not able to haul it in because of the great number of fish."

We've remarked before that Yeshua told them to cast their net on the right side of the boat. This implies they'd been fishing from the other side, the left side. Fishing from the left side is not good, and this has nothing to do with your political position. You may remember that the right side in Jewish thought corresponds with the Torah, God's covenant, and with the concept of water. The left side, on the other hand, is the side of fire (*aish*). The left side is the side of judgment. For this reason, in part, left-handed priests were disqualified from service in the Temple, and in the Temple, you always turned to the right, never to the left. Why? If we approach Him from the place of fire and strict judgment, who would be able to stand and encounter the Lord and His presence? In the house of God, the right side was meaningful. Now, I'm not saying left-handed people today can't serve God or be creative or should try to become right-handed. In the New Covenant the focus is the body and blood of our Messiah and what He did for us. All else is secondary.

But when we live and fish from the left side, our nets will always be empty. To go deeper, we must ask what the right side is. We know the right side is associated with the Word of God. But the right side is also associated with *chesed*, God's loving-kindness. That's God's covenantal love supplied and applied.

We've mentioned that the right side is associated with water as well. *Water* in Hebrew is represented by the thirteenth letter of the Hebrew alphabet, the letter *mem* (מ). The Hebrew alphabet originated in an early Semitic pictograph form, and they wrote the letter *mem* in the shape of waves. From ancient times, the letter *mem* was associated with water and the number 13.

In the Western world, we tend to think of the number 13 as an unlucky number. But 13, from a Jewish Hebraic perspective, is one of the most beloved and significant numbers. Why? Because the Hebrew word for love, *ahava*, has a numerical value of . . . 13. But not only does love equal 13, unity equals 13. Deuteronomy 6:4 says, "Hear O Israel, the LORD our God, the LORD is one." Or, in Hebrew, *Shema Yisrael, Adonai eloheinu, Adonai echad.* The word for one, *echad*, can be understood as *unity* and equals 13. Both the Hebrew words for love and unity equal thirteen. First Corinthians chapter 13 is the "love chapter" in the Bible. The chapter contains thirteen verses, with the last verse, 13:13, saying, "Three things will last forever—faith, hope, and love—and the greatest of these is love" (NLT). I don't believe any of this is mere coincidence, even though there were no chapters and verses in the original Greek manuscript and this chapter was given the number thirteen many years later. Yet God is directing all of it.

## Thirteen Attributes of Mercy

Our big catch will not come until we are made one in love through Messiah.

From a Torah perspective, God has thirteen attributes of mercy. All of them are rooted in His love, which, as we've discussed, also has a numerical value of 13. The thirteen attributes are taken from a passage in Exodus 34:6–7, when the children of Israel rebelled against God and He destroyed them because they sinned with the golden calf. Moses returned to the mountain and hid in the cleft of the rock. In the opinion of Jewish scholars and teachers Rabbenu Tam and David Abudraham, the thirteen attributes are as follows:

- The Lord! (*Adonai*)—God is merciful before a person sins! Even though aware that future evil lies dormant within him.
- The Lord! (*Adonai*)—God is merciful after the sinner has gone astray.
- God (*El*)—a name that denotes power as ruler over nature and humankind, indicating that God's mercy sometimes surpasses even the degree indicated by this name.
- Compassionate (*rahum*)—God is filled with loving sympathy for human frailty, does not put people into situations of extreme temptation, and eases the punishment of the guilty.

- Gracious (*v'hanun*)—God shows mercy even to those who do not deserve it, consoling the afflicted and raising up the oppressed.
- Slow to anger (*ereh apayim*)—God gives the sinner ample time to reflect, improve, and repent.
- Abundant in kindness (*v'rav hesed*)—God is kind toward those who lack personal merits, providing more gifts and blessings than they deserve; if one's personal behavior is evenly balanced between virtue and sin, God tips the scales of justice toward the good.
- Truth (*v'emet*)—God never reneges on His word to reward those who serve Him.
- Preserver of kindness for thousands of generations (*notzeir hesed la-alafim*)—God remembers the deeds of the righteous for the benefit of their less virtuous generations of offspring (thus we constantly invoke the merit of the Patriarchs).
- Forgiver of iniquity (*nosei avon*)—God forgives intentional sin resulting from an evil disposition, as long as the sinner repents.
- Forgiver of willful sin (*pesha*)—God allows even those who commit a sin with the malicious intent of rebelling against and angering Him the opportunity to repent.
- Forgiver of error (*v'hata'ah*)—God forgives a sin committed out of carelessness, thoughtlessness, or apathy.
- Who cleanses (*v'nakeh*)—God is merciful, gracious, and forgiving, wiping away the sins of those who truly repent; however, if one does not repent, God does not cleanse.[3]

During the High Holidays—Rosh Hashanah, the Feast of Trumpets, and *Yom Kippur*—we recite these thirteen attributes of mercy as we ask

God to do with us according to them. We ask Him to deal with us from the right side, not the left side.

Below are other fascinating facts relating to the number 13:

YHVH/the Lord equals 26 (13 x 2)

The Lord is One/YHVH Echad equals 39 (13 x 3)

The value of the Shema (Deut. 6:4) is 1,118 (13 x 86)

Messiah/Mashiach equals 358, and Moses equals 345. The
    difference is 13.

Messiah was going to demonstrate love and loving-kindness well beyond Moses. Moses loved the people and risked his life to intercede for them. Messiah, though, gave His life for us. He lived from the right side and is the fulfillment of thirteen. While we await His return in love and loving-kindness, we also need to seek full nets through the power of the Holy Spirit, prayer, and His Word.

## Strengthened by Love and Unity

The key to seeing the great catch and a great revival movement of God is love and loving-kindness. It's through these two conduits the Messiah moves and is going to come. If we are not unified by our love for one another, our nets will break. Until we come into relational unity as Jew and Gentile, or come into relational unity with the people that God brings into our lives, we will not see the fullness of God's blessing. Husbands and wives, families, communities, and churches need to be unified for our nets to be full and not break. This unity must be rooted in love, because the nets are only as strong as the knots that bind them together.

The knots represent our connections through the relationships God puts in our lives.

In Luke 5:10, Yeshua called Peter to follow Him after Peter obediently cast his net at Yeshua's word, and the catch was so large the nets were breaking. Commenting on this verse, the *Pulpit Commentary* says, "Augustine beautifully compares the broken and torn net to **the Church that now is**, full of divisions and rents; the net unrent and untorn will be the **Church of the future**, which will know no schisms."⁴

The net symbolizes the network of covenantal Kingdom relationships and partnerships that the Lord is bringing together at this season. No individual or ministry can create a net that is big enough or strong enough to contain what God wants to do. Historically the nets of revival break because people want to make their own nets. They want to manage the moves of God and lay claim to what He is doing. Revivals are quenched when they become "all about me" instead of all about God's sovereignty.

I believe the Lord is waiting for enough nets to join in unity before He sends the great catch. We can't have the catch without the container (nets that don't break). The container is only for the sake of the catch God provides.

This joining is a lot like a group of companies joining together. I fly a lot, and in my travels I've encountered a group of airlines that have come together under the banner of oneworld Alliance. Their website says, "Our world-class airlines have come together to provide the highest level of service and smoothest connections to more than 900 destinations in 170 territories. From check-in to security and boarding, oneworld member airlines work together to make your flying experience as seamless as possible."⁵ These airlines have joined as commercial "nets" that allow us to fly more easily. No single airline can cover every destination, so they have come together, in unity, to serve their customers. Friends, this is how we fulfill the Great Commission. We must set aside our differences and band together to tell people about Messiah Yeshua. We must make it easier for people to embrace Him and learn from Him how to live in this crazy world. And we do that together.

The Bible gives us a clear idea of what love and relational unity look like on a corporate level. These are Yeshua's words in John 17:20–23:

> I pray not on behalf of these only, but also for those who believe in Me through their message, that they all may be one. Just as You, Father, are in Me and I am in You, so also may they be one in Us, so the world may believe that You sent Me. The glory that You have given to Me I have given to them, that they may be one just as We are one—I in them and You in Me—that they may be perfected in unity, so that the world may know that You sent Me and loved them as You loved Me.

When we become one, we are perfected in unity. Then the world will know the Father sent Yeshua. When Jews and Gentiles unite, we become perfected, and we grow into the fullness of maturity. We need each other, Jew and Gentile. Corporate unity leads to fulfilling Yeshua's purpose.

Let me be clear about something. The source of our unity is God. But unity is not uniformity. We each have different roles and functions. We each play our part. Unity celebrates diversity because love binds unity.

Jesus prays for unity—one people of God around a common purpose to achieve God's mission. This requires balance: we need to be careful not to place unity above His Word, and at the same time be careful not to become exclusionary. Jesus wants us to be one. Our unity will lead directly to people being saved. Psalm 133:1 tells us, "How good and how pleasant it is for brothers to dwell together in unity!" To have full nets, and to pull in the catch of blessings, we have to live from a place of love and relational unity.

God's presence, power, and provision is always proportional to the unity of God's people. We need to unite and form the nets that won't break in preparation for the great catch that is coming.

These professional fishermen learned quite a lesson from Messiah. If they were to experience all God had for them as "fishers of men," they needed to follow what Yeshua said. They needed to think differently. They needed to realize that disunity would break their nets and they'd lose fish (people, blessings, provision).

John 21 gives us a glimpse into our lives as well. Are we willing to shift our focus to the other side of the boat? Fishermen know how to work, but it takes faith to fill our nets to overflowing.

# TEN

# IS IT POSSIBLE TO DO
# MIRACLES TODAY?

In this book, we've read about many biblical miracles, from turning water into wine to healing and provision. I've also shared personal accounts where I've witnessed God move miraculously. Now I want to ask you a question. Are miracles still possible today? I believe they are. I also believe that God wants you to trust that they are possible and for that to impact you and how you live your life.

Not too long ago, a friend called me to pray for one of her friends who had leukemia. The doctors were concerned about his rapid decline and didn't know if he would make it. As we prayed, I felt God's tangible presence wrap around me. Shortly afterward, she wrote me the following email:

I'm sitting at the computer, praising God because Gustavo is sitting right next to me. He was released from the hospital on Thursday. Just wanted to let you know a few miracles that have taken place since you began to pray last Shabbat. He was near death last Saturday. No one can explain what happened to him and why. The doctors can't explain why a serious condition (low blood cell count) that usually lasts between 9–12 days lasted only 12 hours. (The day you started praying.) His lowest white blood cell was 1300. Now it is normal (over 8500). Praise Yeshua!!!!!!!!!!!!!!!!!!!!!!!!!!! Thank you for your willingness to be of service to the God of Israel and caring for the sick!!! We are attaching a picture of us taken today!!!

What a wonderful example of how God still moves today in response to prayer. This was a miracle that even the doctors couldn't figure out. I love when that happens. In addition, it was an astonishing testimony to my Jewish friend of the power of Yeshua. Truly, God is doing extraordinary things in the world today and wants you and me to be part of that.

God's will is clear. Yeshua taught us to pray, "Your kingdom come, your will be done on earth as it is in heaven" (Matt. 6:10). That phrase from the Lord's Prayer isn't some wishy-washy prayer for the future that is up for debate. God calls us to pray for the Kingdom and then live it out in demonstration. His will is to bring heaven to earth to establish His Kingdom in part now and in full when He returns. A fundamental biblical principle declares that the end days will look like the beginning, or as it was in the beginning (Isa. 46:10). As believers, God calls us to look to Yeshua and His early followers and emulate them. God is pouring out His presence and power today just as He did in the book of Acts, only in a more splendid measure. His followers, then, should be our role models.

## Yeshua's Miracles Set Him Apart

As I've written in other chapters, Yeshua's miracles demonstrated that He was a prophet like Moses. Deuteronomy 18:18 reminds us, "I will raise up a prophet like you for them from among their brothers." Yeshua performed more incredible miracles than Moses and was set apart because of those. The power and authority in which He operated both astonished and convicted people. Matthew 7:28–29 underscores the point: "Now when *Yeshua* had finished these words, the crowds were astounded at His teaching, for He was teaching them as one having authority and not as their *Torah* scholars." Yeshua taught with *power* and *authority*, and He operated in a way that resulted in *miracles*. These three attributes demonstrated the proof of His message and set Him apart. It also sparked jealousy in the self-righteous teachers and rabbis.

## Not for Yeshua Alone

Yeshua wasn't the only one who performed miracles. He granted that power and authority to His disciples. The good news is, when we are born again, Yeshua grants that same power and authority to us. We can perform miracles too! Some might think, *Miracles are for Yeshua and the apostles, but that period has ended.* I know that is not true because I've experienced miracles in my life and ministry. Operating in the supernatural and experiencing miracles is also for us today. Yeshua said, "Amen, amen I tell you, he who puts his trust in Me, the works that I do he will do; and greater than these he will do, because I am going to the Father" (John 14:12). This is a remarkable statement! Yeshua said that we could do works that are not only like His but potentially even greater than the ones He did. I realize when we read those words, they seem impossible. How can we possibly do miracles on the level of Yeshua or even more remarkable? No way! I'm just a flawed human, right?

Remember, Yeshua was God incarnate. "And the Word became flesh and tabernacled among us," wrote John. "We looked upon His glory, the glory of the one and only from the Father, full of grace and truth" (John 1:14). Yeshua was the Word that became flesh, God made manifest in human form. Yeshua operated in supernatural wisdom, revelation, power, and authority—100 percent human and 100 percent divine. Yeshua was the only 200 percent person who has ever existed. So it makes sense that He could do supernatural signs and wonders. Yes, there's quite a big difference between Yeshua and us. So how can we credibly be close to His miracles? Yeshua's statement in John 14:12 doesn't make sense unless we grasp the nugget of truth within it.

To help us understand, let's read what the apostle and rabbi Paul wrote in Philippians 2:5–8:

> Have this attitude in yourselves, which also was in Messiah *Yeshua*, Who, though existing in the form of God, did not consider being equal to God a thing to be grasped. But He emptied Himself—taking on the form of a slave, becoming the likeness of men and being found in appearance as a man. He humbled Himself—becoming obedient to the point of death, even death on a cross.

Many commentators and scholars refer to this as the *kenosis* doctrine. It comes from the Greek word meaning "to empty." Yeshua emptied Himself of His divinity. He did His miracles out of His humanity, not His divinity. This doctrine and Scripture are a key part of the answer as to why *we* can do more extraordinary things.

### Authority and Power to Minister

Yeshua did not perform a single miracle until after His immersion, commonly referred to as His baptism, by John the Immerser. Luke 3:21–22 tells us,

> Now when all the people were immersed, *Yeshua* also was immersed. And while He was praying, heaven was opened and the *Ruach*

*ha-Kodesh [Holy Spirit]* came down upon Him in bodily form like a dove. And from out of heaven came a voice, "You are My Son, whom I love—with You I am well pleased!"

When Yeshua was immersed, He was filled with the Holy Spirit. Now let's look at the next chapter in Luke:

*Yeshua*, now filled with the *Ruach ha-Kodesh*, returned from the Jordan. He was led by the *Ruach* in the wilderness for forty days, being tested by the devil. Now He ate nothing during those days, and when they had ended, He was hungry. (4:1–2)

*Yeshua* returned in the power of the *Ruach* to the Galilee, and news about Him went out through all the surrounding region. He taught in their synagogues, and everyone was praising Him. (4:14–15)

Yeshua was tested in the wilderness and then, being filled with the Holy Spirit, He returned to the Galilee and began preaching and teaching with power and authority. The word about Him spread to other regions. There's a definite order to His ability to do miracles.

### Why Forty Days?

Forty is the number of preparation. Moses' life was broken up into three forty-year periods of preparation:

- Forty years in Egypt in Pharaoh's house, preparing him for . . .
- forty years as a shepherd, preparing him for . . .
- the last forty years—leading the Children of Israel in the wilderness wanderings and ultimately preparing them to go into the Promised Land.

Moses spent two-thirds of his life preparing for the third forty-year period. He was 120 years old when he died. Moses also spent forty days in the presence of God on Mount Sinai. Yeshua spent forty days in the wilderness. This period points to Him as a second Moses preparing for His mission. Israel was prepared and tested for forty years in the wilderness before entering the Promised Land. The Lord always tests us before He blesses us. Yeshua passed the test. After He left the wilderness, word about Him spread, and He began His ministry of teaching and miracles.

The number forty also connects to Yeshua's preparation of the disciples and the promise of supernatural power and authority for His followers. We read about this in Acts 1:1–5:

> I wrote the first volume, Theophilus, about all that *Yeshua* began to do and teach—up to the day He was taken up, after He had given orders by the *Ruach ha-Kodesh* to the emissaries He had chosen. To them He showed Himself to be alive after His suffering through many convincing proofs, appearing to them **for forty days and speaking about the kingdom of God**. Now while staying with them, He commanded them not to leave Jerusalem, but to wait for what the Father promised—which, He said, "you heard from Me. For John immersed with water, but you will be immersed in the *Ruach ha-Kodesh* not many days from now." (emphasis mine)

John immersed with water, but what would become more critical was their immersion in the Holy Spirit. Luke continued:

> So when they gathered together, they asked Him, "Lord, are You restoring the kingdom to Israel at this time?" He said to them, "It is not your place to know the times or seasons which the Father has

placed under His own control. But you will receive power when the *Ruach ha-Kodesh* has come upon you; and you will be My witnesses in Jerusalem, and through all Judah, and Samaria, and to the end of the earth." (1:6–8)

Yeshua taught and prepared the disciples. Part of that preparation was purifying them of their fears, misconceptions, and wrong beliefs. He taught them about the Kingdom before He ascended on the fortieth day after His resurrection. On that fortieth day, Yeshua promised them they would be witnesses and receive power when the Holy Spirit came upon them so they could testify to who He was.

That teaching and preparation has never changed and is for all of Yeshua's disciples, including us. What God did for them, He wants to do for *you*. John 1:32–34 reminds us that the greater immersion came through Yeshua! John wrote:

> I have seen the *Ruach* coming down like a dove out of heaven, and it remained on Him. I did not know Him; but the One who sent me to immerse in water said to me, "The One on whom you see the *Ruach* coming down and remaining, this is the One who immerses in the *Ruach ha-Kodesh [Holy Spirit]*." And I have seen and testified that this is *Ben-Elohim [Son of God]*.

John testified that the One whom he immersed in water would immerse in the Holy Spirit. We also find this idea in the book of Acts. Rabbi Paul came across some of John the Immerser's disciples. John's disciples only knew about water immersion, not immersion in the Holy Spirit that comes from faith in Yeshua. At that point, they believed and were immersed and filled with the Holy Spirit (Acts 19:1–6).

# Power and Authority

With the filling of the Holy Spirit, there is the promise of power and authority for your life. I love this definition from pastor John Wimber: "Power is the ability, the strength and the might to complete a given task. Authority is the right to use the power of God."[1]

We need to remember that the context of Acts 1 and 2 is Pentecost. Pentecost celebrates Moses bringing the Torah at Mount Sinai. Even more significant than that, however, is that Yeshua promised to give a greater gift—the gift of the Holy Spirit. It's an equally incredible gift. We need both the Word and the Spirit. However, in some ways, it's more fantastic because the Spirit of God in us illuminates God's Word, allowing us to interpret and apply it. Israel struggled to keep God's Word, but we are empowered in a way they never were by the Holy Spirit dwelling inside us.

Power is like a gun, and a badge represents the authority to use it. Criminals can have guns and do horrible things, as we've seen in our nation. They have the gun and the power, but they don't have the authority like police officers or the military. Yeshua wants to deputize and empower you. You have been called, appointed, and given a position of authority in the Kingdom. You're anointed, and He's given you the power.

The purpose of giving us power and authority is to fulfill God's initial calling at Mount Sinai to be a royal priesthood and a holy nation. In the Hebrew Scriptures, prophets, priests, and kings received the Holy Spirit. In 1 Samuel 10, the prophet Samuel anointed King Saul, and the Spirit of God came upon him. Saul began to prophesy (v. 10). First Samuel 10:11 tells us, "So when all who knew him formerly saw him prophesying with the prophets, they said one to another, 'What has happened to the son of

Kish? Is Saul also among the prophets?'" This anointing and receiving of the Spirit allowed Saul to serve God.

Without the Holy Spirit, we can't fulfill our destiny as God's people and His royal priesthood. It's also impossible to walk in the anointing in our personal lives and callings. Trying to fulfill God's purposes in our strength invariably leads to frustration and burnout. Saturation of the Holy Spirit leads to maturation. Considering Luke 4 again, we see in verses 31–37 that early in Yeshua's ministry, He cast an unclean spirit out of a man in the Capernaum synagogue. Yeshua rebuked the spirit, saying,

> "Quiet! Come out of him!" And when the demon threw him down in their midst, it came out without hurting him. They were all amazed, and they spoke to one another, saying, "What is this message? **For with authority and power** He commands the unclean spirits, and they come out." So His reputation grew, spreading to every place in that region. (emphasis mine)

## Power and Authority Delegated

After Yeshua cast out the demons, the people were amazed by His power and authority because the evil spirits were subject to Him. Then, in Luke 9:1–6, Yeshua called His twelve disciples and gave *them* power and authority over demons and to cure diseases. Yeshua has power and authority, and He delegated that power and authority to His disciples.

Let's not forget what I wrote earlier. Power and authority for followers of Yeshua is a certainty. The delegation of power isn't just limited to the twelve. The baton of delegation has been passed down to us. Matthew wrote,

And *Yeshua* came up to them and spoke to them, saying, "All authority in heaven and on earth has been given to Me. Go therefore and make disciples of all nations, immersing them in the name of the Father and the Son and the *Ruach ha-Kodesh*, teaching them to observe all I have commanded you. And remember! I am with you always, even to the end of the age." (28:18–20)

Yeshua's words are great news! He is with us until the end. That's why John 14:11–14 is so important. Verse 12 says, "The person who trusts me will not only do what I'm doing but even greater things, because I, on my way to the Father, am giving you the same work to do that I've been doing. You can count on it" (MSG). These greater works are not only for the disciples but also for you and me.

It's disheartening that most churches have settled for weak faith. Many believers live way below the level of fullness God desires for them, experiencing a life full of frustration, weariness, and uncertainty. It's half a Gospel. We proclaim the Gospel of salvation and help people know Messiah, and yet we fail to demonstrate the Gospel of the Kingdom that comes in power and authority rooted in our royal priestly identity as His sons and daughters. We can't forget Yeshua's prayer was, "Your kingdom come, Your will be done on earth as it is in heaven" (Matt. 6:10). Bringing the Kingdom and the good news to earth is God's will for us. Yet it's not something we must strive to do or make happen. We have the power and authority!

Rabbi Paul wrote, "For we are His workmanship—created in Messiah *Yeshua* for good deeds, which God prepared beforehand so we might walk in them" (Eph. 2:10). God equips and enables us to fulfill the assignments and good things that He prepared in advance for us to do.

Part of that is supernatural. This is underscored by Acts 4:12–14:

"There is salvation in no one else, for there is no other name under heaven given to mankind by which we must be saved!" Now when they saw the boldness of Peter and John and figured out they were laymen without training, they were amazed. They began to realize that these men had been with *Yeshua*. But seeing the healed man standing with them, they had nothing to say in response.

These men were uneducated, as many evaluate education, but they knew the Scriptures and had spent time in Yeshua's presence. They had an intimate relationship with Him. Their power and authority could come only from the Messiah Yeshua. In an earlier chapter, we examined the healing at the pool of Bethesda. The man had been lame from birth for thirty-eight years, and Yeshua healed him on Pentecost. This is significant, and in Acts 4, we find the disciples following in Yeshua's footsteps—and so can we. What does this tell us?

- This unique power and authority *only* flow out of a unique and intimate relationship with the Lord.
- What is true for Yeshua, and true for the disciples, is also true for us!
- Cultivating a unique, intimate relationship with Him leads to extraordinary power and authority, allowing us to perform the works of the Kingdom.

How can we be passionate about the message and not feel ashamed or defeated? Acts 4:33 tells us, "With great power the apostles continued to testify to the resurrection of the Lord Jesus. And God's grace was so powerfully at work in them all" (NIV). This verse is one of the keys to the supernatural power to proclaim the good news of the Messiah and not feel defeated, because it's His power and authority working through us, not our own.

## Power and Authority Means Several Things

Most think that the good news is restricted to believing in Yeshua and that they'll go to heaven one day. They feel that their life will be difficult until they see heaven. That's a falsehood. God doesn't want your life to be terrible until you go to heaven. I'm not saying there won't be hard times or testing. Yeshua Himself said, "In the world you will have tribulation; but be of good cheer, I have overcome the world" (John 16:33 NKJV). Of course, going to heaven is good news! It's wonderful and life-changing news that our sins are cleansed, and we are new creatures in Yeshua. Yet there's so much more as we live in Yeshua's power and authority. Eternal life doesn't start when we die and go to heaven. It starts the moment we are born again. Part of eternal life is walking in all God has for us.

## The Supernatural Ability and Power to Heal and Make Whole

Miracles were critical for the growth of the early community of faith. The apostles healed many. You can read about it in the books of Acts (2:43–45; 5:12) and Mark (16:16–20). But this ability and power are not limited to them—they can transform your life.

A young woman had been extremely sick for some time, and her friends brought her to me. She was suffering from Hashimoto's disease, an autoimmune disorder that causes numerous issues, including severe food allergies, fatigue, and blood and stomach complications. Many people had prayed for her, but her condition only worsened. Because she had not experienced any improvement after the previous prayers, she was reluctant for anyone else to pray for her. Discouraged and feeling there was not much hope left, she didn't want me to pray for her. Fortunately, her friends refused to give up and convinced her to allow me to pray for her. After our prayer time together, she felt the overwhelming presence of God over her and knew He had healed her. Then she went out and did something that astonished her family. She ate Mexican food, which would usually make her extremely sick and cause horrible pain. But God *had* healed her of all these things and made her well—no sickness or pain.

There's something I want all of us to remember. This young woman had to risk being prayed for, and I had to take the risk of praying for her, believing God could touch her. I certainly didn't want to be yet another one of those disappointments, and by God's grace, He answered our prayers.

Our Fusion Global ministry has witnessed so many healing miracles, from diabetes to leukemia. We've seen a girl put down her crutches and walk as God healed her muscular dystrophy. We can pray for people. God can use us, and we can see people healed and made whole. But we must believe God.

Unfortunately, not everyone we pray for will get well, because we live in the tension between the "not yet" Kingdom and the "fulfilled" Kingdom. The Kingdom has come in part, and genuine healing is available. God does miracles in people's lives, but at the same time, because we're not fully in the Kingdom, we're not going to see every person healed. But we must believe and always pray with faith because we love and serve a sovereign God. We must take the risk and step out in faithful prayer.

# The Supernatural Ability and Power
# to Hear God's Voice

Yeshua said, "My sheep hear My voice. I know them, and they follow Me. I give them eternal life! They will never perish, and no one will snatch them out of My hand" (John 10:27–28). God designed us to hear His voice. Adam and Eve clearly communicated with God in the Garden. Unfortunately, the Fall hindered our ability to hear Him. Yeshua, however, came and restored what the first man and woman had broken. God wants to speak. We must take the time to learn how to tune in.

When we follow Yeshua and come to faith, He begins to fix our hearing. This supernatural fixing is significant because hearing leads to healing and greater wholeness. The inability to hear hinders our healing because we need the voice of God through the Scriptures. His still, small voice speaks to us in a variety of ways. Hearing God's voice brings healing and wholeness on an emotional and relational level. In addition, God wants us to hear not just for ourselves but for others as well.

We see the example of hearing for others in the story of the Samaritan woman at the well. After her encounter with Yeshua, she returned to her Samaritan village exclaiming, "Come see a man who told me everything I ever did! He couldn't be the Messiah, could He?" (John 4:29). Scripture goes on to tell us that "the people left town and began coming to Him" (v. 30). What compelled her to proclaim with such enthusiasm, to come to meet a man who told her everything she ever did? This Samaritan woman felt seen and known for the first time in her life after the power of Yeshua's words. Carrying a load of guilt and shame for years, she had been looked down on and judged by many. Now through a word from God, she was set free. God wants to use us in the same capacity to speak life and healing into others, often through a word from the Holy Spirit.

Once, another young woman came up to me after I taught at a faith-based entertainment conference. She told me about how a famous producer wanted to cast her in a movie. However, this movie was about an ungodly individual connected to wicked events. She told the producer she couldn't do it. The producer was shocked because this movie could have been her big break. He asked her why she declined the role. "Well, I'm a Christian," she told him. Those words led to incredible conversations and an opportunity for her to share the Gospel with him. Her story had a positive effect on me. As I prayed for her and blessed her, I felt prompted by the Holy Spirit to tell her what the Lord was saying: "You are going to work with Oprah Winfrey." I knew nothing about her, so this was a real risk. I mean, what are the odds? Miraculously, just like the Lord had said, she wound up working with Oprah and was in several of her TV shows on Oprah's network. This was an explicit confirmation that the Lord still speaks directly today. It's about opening your ears to God and allowing Him to speak to you. God wants us to be vessels that He can speak through to impact other people's lives. It's incredible, but we must listen for His voice. I do want to pause and say that the written Word of God, the Scriptures, are the final plumb line for all truth. When the Holy Spirit speaks to our hearts, He will never violate the written Word of God. If what we feel does contradict, then it is not from God.

Once, while in Israel, I sensed God give me a message for someone. While we were immersing, a person came, and I told him, "Your spouse is struggling with alcohol addiction." Again, that was a risk. Then I told him that God would heal them and restore their marriage. It was all true, and God did what He said.

I love to take people to Israel, immerse them in love, and hear God's voice about families being healed and restored and all sorts of incredible miracles and blessings.

These few stories illustrate the power and authority to hear God's voice for yourself and others.

## The Supernatural Power and Authority to Bless

There is a difference between praying and blessing. In Jewish thought, praying is for things that are not. Blessing is asking God to multiply what is. I mentioned this in the chapter on the miracle of multiplication. Yeshua blessed the bread and the fish, and they were multiplied.

In the same way, you have the power to bless. You have the power to bless your family. I love to bless my children at *Shabbat* and call forth their identity and destiny. I believe that has impacted them and marked and changed them. One of my family members was having a difficult time, and I prayed and asked for a blessing. I'm the high priest of this family, and in that power and authority, I commanded that the attack stop and go back. We can go directly to Yeshua's throne and ask Him to deal with issues and bless others.

You can bless your family, friends, home, and possessions. I do believe that there's power in that blessing.

Yeshua said you could do greater things than these. He performed miracles not in His divinity but rather operated as an unfallen man anointed by the Spirit. Yeshua has also said *you* can do the greater things, and that's my encouragement. Take risks and step out in faith. Pray, bless, and watch what the Lord does, even if it takes one hundred or a thousand times. God is faithful. I'm sure if you, by faith, continue seeking and asking, you will eventually have the answer to your prayers, maybe in some unexpected, God-directed way.

# ACKNOWLEDGMENTS

This book would not be possible without the support of my family. I am so blessed to have such a fantastic "tribe" who goes above and beyond.

Miriam, thank you for all your love and encouragement! I love being on this journey with you.

Avi and Judah, I love you and am blessed to be your dad. I am grateful for our adventures and the joy of seeing God's hand on your lives.

Mom and Dad, I could not ask for better parents. The boys and I are so blessed by all you do for our family. Dad, you're my hero!

Aunt Carol, thank you for being like a second mom, for always believing in me and cheering me on.

Aunt Wendy, thanks for being like a big sister. I always love spending time with you, Uncle Alex, and Sabrina.

Ted Squires, you are an actual "God send"! I am deeply thankful for you and Terry. You are more than a friend—you are family!

Thanks to everyone on the Fusion Global Team. Each of you has helped me make a more significant impact for Yeshua than I could have on my own! Specials thanks to Alicia, Drew, Rabbi Ryan, Mark, Kesha, Wayne, and Max.

Thanks to everyone on the W Publishing Team. Special thanks to Damon, Kyle, Caren, and Allison. You all are amazing! I so appreciate your faith in this project and all your hard work.

# NOTES

## Introduction

1. The "before you begin" section is excerpted in part from Rabbi Jason's book *Mysteries of the Messiah* (Nashville, TN: Thomas Nelson, 2021).
2. Here's how the Hebrew numeric system works: the first ten Hebrew letters increase in value by a factor of one (*aleph* is 1, *bet* is 2, and so on). The next ten Hebrew letters increase in value by a factor of ten (*kaf* is 20, *lamed* is 30, and so on). The final Hebrew letters increase in value by a factor of one hundred (*kof* is 100, *reish* is 200, and so on) through the final letter, *tav*, with a value of 400.
3. Stringed instruments (Ps. 4:1), wind instruments (Ps. 5:1), Gittite lyre (Ps. 8:1), *machalatle' anot* (Ps. 88:1, Hebrew version), Yedu Sun (Ps. 39:1), lyre and harp (Ps. 33:2), and the eight voices of the singers.
4. Lois Tverberg, "Can We Use Jewish Sources to Study Jesus?" *Our Rabbi Jesus: Insights from Lois Tverberg* (blog), November 28, 2012, https://ourrabbijesus.com /articles/can-we-use-jewish-sources-to-study-jesus.

## Chapter 1: The Signs and Secrets of Transformation

1. Barney Kasdan, *God's Appointed Customs: A Messianic Jewish Guide to the Biblical Lifecycle and Lifestyle* (Baltimore, MD: Messianic Jewish Publishers, 1996), 48.
2. Rabbi Aaron L. Raskin, "Nun, the Fourteenth Letter of the Hebrew Alphabet," Chabad.org, accessed December 13, 2022, https://www.chabad.org/library /article_cdo/aid/137086/jewish/Nun.htm.
3. Ellen Frankel and Betsy Platkin Teutsch, *The Encyclopedia of Jewish Symbols* (New York: Rowman & Littlefield, 1995), 77.
4. Rabbi Alfred J. Kolatch, *The Jewish Book of Why* (Middle Village, NY: Jonathan Davie Publishers, 1981), 35.

5. John Sailhamer, *The Pentateuch as Narrative: A Biblical-Theological Commentary* (Grand Rapids, MI: Zondervan, 1995), 129.

6. Helen Keller, quoted in Marcus A. Roberts, *Thoughts for Your Day: Meditations Food for Contemplation* (Bloomington, IN: AuthorHouse, 2019), e-book.

7. William Barclay, *The Gospel of John*, revised and updated., vol. 1, *The New Daily Study Bible* (Edinburgh: Saint Andrew Press, 2001), 119.

8. Jessica LaGrone, *The Miracles of Jesus: Finding God in Desperate Moments* (Nashville, TN: Abingdon Press, 2017), e-book edition.

9. "Chutzpah Definition and Meaning—The Origins and Connotations," Jewish Shop, June 17, 2020, https://jewish.shop/35454/chutzpah-definition/.

10. See 1 Corinthians 15:21–22, 45–49; Romans 5:12–15, 17.

11. *The William Davidson Talmud* (Koren–Steinsaltz), Berakhot 34b, https://www.sefaria.org/Berakhot.34b.24?ven=William_Davidson_Edition_-_English&vhe=William_Davidson_Edition_-_Vocalized_Aramaic&lang=bi&with=all&lang2=en.

## Chapter 2: The Signs and Secrets of Purification

1. My book *Aligning with God's Appointed Times* has more details about Passover and all the biblical holidays. It's available from Amazon or Fusionglobal.org.

2. This forms the background of what Rabbi Paul wrote in 1 Corinthians 5:6–8.

3. *The William Davidson Talmud* (Koren–Steinsaltz), Berakhot 17a, https://www.sefaria.org/Berakhot.17a.2?ven=William_Davidson_Edition_-_English&vhe=William_Davidson_Edition_-_Vocalized_Aramaic&lang=bi.

4. Zohar Shemos, 40, Riya Mehema as quoted in Eliyahu Kitov, *The Heritage Haggadah*, trans. Gershon Robinson (Nanuet, NY: Feldheim Publishers Jerusalem, 1999), 5.

5. Aaron L. Raskin, "Moses and Pharaoh, Good and Bad Speech: Parsha Va'eira," Chabad.org, accessed March 20, 2023, https://www.chabad.org/multimedia/audio_cdo/aid/1872413/jewish/Moses-and-Pharaoh-Good-and-Bad-Speech.htm.

6. For more on burning the leaven, see the article written by Eliyahu Kitov, "Search, Removal, and Burning of Chametz," Chabad.org, accessed March 20, 2023, https://www.chabad.org/holidays/passover/pesach_cdo/aid/1744/jewish/Search-Removal-and-Burning-of-Chametz.htm.

7. Joshua Kulp, "Pirkei Avot 1:2," accessed May 14, 2023, https://www.sefaria.org/Pirkei_Avot.1.2?lang=bi.

8. Shraga Silverstein, "Mishnah Shekalim 1:3," accessed May 14, 2023, https://www.sefaria.org/Mishnah_Shekalim.1.3?ven=The_Mishna_with_Obadiah_Bartenura_by_Rabbi_Shraga_Silverstein&lang=bi.

9. *The William Davidson Talmud* (Koren–Steinsaltz), Megillah 29b, https://www.sefaria.org/Megillah.29b?lang=bi.

## Chapter 3: The Signs and Secrets of New Birth

1. Cited in Shaye J. D. Cohen, *From the Maccabees to the Mishnah,* 2nd ed. (Louisville, KY: Westminster John Knox Press, 2006), 264.

2. A. Andrew Das, "Sadducees," in *The Lexham Bible Dictionary,* ed. John D. Barry et al. (Bellingham, WA: Lexham Press, 2016).

3. Rabbi Jonathan Sacks, "Argument for the Sake of Heaven," Chabad.org, accessed January 5, 2023, https://www.chabad.org/parshah/article_cdo/aid/4422484 /jewish/Argument-for-the-Sake-of-Heaven.htm.

4. *The William Davidson Talmud* (Koren–Steinsaltz), Gittin 56a, https://www .sefaria.org/Gittin.56a.8?lang=bi&with=all&lang2=en; *The William Davidson Talmud* (Koren–Steinsaltz), Taanit 19b:15, https://www.sefaria.org/Taanit .19b.15?lang=bi&with=all&lang2=en; and Rabbi Shraga Silverstein, Sifrei Devarim 305:4, https://www.sefaria.org/Sifrei_Devarim.305.4?lang=bi.

5. *The William Davidson Talmud,* "Avot D'Rabbi Natan 6," 2019, https://www .sefaria.org/Avot_D'Rabbi_Natan.6.3?lang=bi&with=all&lang2=en.

6. See also Matt. 8:12; 25:30; 2 Peter 2:17; Rev. 16:10.

7. Job 1:22.

## Chapter 4: The Signs and Secrets of the Serpent

1. *Targum Jerusalem*, Deuteronomy 30.12–14:12.

2. J. W. Etheridge, *The Targums of Onkelos and Jonathan Ben Uzziel on the Pentateuch: Leviticus, Numbers, and Deuteronomy* (London: Longman, Green, Longman, and Roberts, 1865), 654.

3. In biblical and Jewish thought, going up to Jerusalem is making *aliyah*, which means to ascend or go up. It's the reason the pilgrims who went to worship in the Temple would sing the psalms of ascent (Psalms 112–118). Today when a Jewish person returns to Israel, it's also referred to as making *aliyah* as it's a physical and spiritual ascent. When God gathers His people to Jerusalem, they are making a physical and spiritual ascent, *aliyah*.

4. *Targum Jerusalem*, Deuteronomy 30.3–4.

5. Bill Federer, "Early Astronomers: Mathematics Is the Language in Which God Has Written the Universe," *World Tribune*, August 25, 2018, https://worldtribune .com/life/early-astronomers-mathematics-is-the-language-in-which-god-has -written-the-universe/.

## Chapter 5: The Signs and Secrets of Healing

1. Cited in Denise Lorenz, *Be Free from Fear: Overcoming Fear to Live Free* (Life Changer Press, 2013), eBook edition.

2. "The Bethesda Pool, Site of One of Jesus' Miracles," Biblical Archaeology Society, accessed January 6, 2023, https://www.biblicalarchaeology.org/daily

/biblical-sites-places/jerusalem/the-bethesda-pool-site-of-one-of-jesus
-miracles/.

3. "Abraham, Isaac and Jacob: A Chronology," British Bible School, August 29, 2015, http://britishbibleschool.com/biblos/abraham-isaac-and-jacob-a-chronology.

4. Hayim Nahman Bialik and Yehoshua Hana Ravnitzky ed. and trans. William G. Braude, *The Book of Legends, Sefer Ha-Aggadah: Legends from the Talmud and Midrash* (New York: Schocken Books, 1992), 78.

5. Rabbi Bradley Shavit Artson, "God's Healing Angels," American Jewish University, June 11, 2005, https://www.aju.edu/ziegler-school-rabbinic-studies /our-torah/back-issues/gods-healing-angels.

6. Rabbi Judith HaLevy, "Torah Portion: We All Stood at Sinai," *Jewish Journal*, January 27, 2016, https://jewishjournal.com/judaism/181663/.

7. Rabbi Denise L. Eger, "The Revelation at Sinai Views from the Midrash Shavuot, Legends of the Jews 3:2:18," accessed May 15, 2023, https://www.sefaria.org/sheets /409283.1?lang=bi&with=all&lang2=en.

8. Rabbi Artson, "God's Healing Angels."

## Chapter 6: The Signs and Secrets of Wholeness

1. Zohar 1:119a and 2:7b.

2. "What Is Christian Redemption? What Does It Mean to Be Redeemed?" Compelling Truth, accessed March 22, 2023, https://www.compellingtruth.org /Christian-redemption.html.

3. J. Immanuel Schochet, *Living with Moshiach: Va'eira II* (Brooklyn, NY: Kehot Publication Society, 1999), e-book edition.

4. Vayikra Rabbah 29:1.

5. Rabbi Yitzchak Shurin, "Pesach: Commemorating Freedom of Speech," Yeshiva University, accessed March 22, 2023, https://darchenoam.org/pesach -commemorating-freedom-of-speech/.

6. Rabbi Reuven Chaim Klein, "The Pharaoh and the King," Ohr.edu, January 6, 2018, https://ohr.edu/7666.

## Chapter 7: The Signs and Secrets of Multiplication

1. "The History of Hanukkah," My Jewish Learning, accessed January 7, 2023, https://www.myjewishlearning.com/article/hanukkah-history/.

2. "May 12, 1948 Azzam Pasha, Secretary General of the Arab League," Center for Online Judaic Studies, accessed March 22, 2023, http://cojs.org/ may-12–1948-azzam-pasha-secretary-general-of-the-arab-league/.

3. Rabbi Ephraim Shore, "The Miracle of Israel," April 24, 2022, https://aish.com/ the-miracle-of-israel/.

4. *Pirkei Avot*, 3:21.

5. Eugene H. Peterson and Peter Santucci, *Eat This Book Study Guide* (Grand Rapids, MI: Eerdmans, 2006), 5.

6. Rabbi Ismar Schorsch, "Torah like Water," My Jewish Learning, accessed January 9, 2023,

7. https://www.myjewishlearning.com/article/torah-like-water/.

8. Ariela Pelaia, "Leviathan in Jewish Legend and the Bible," Learn Religions, updated February 4, 2019, https://www.learnreligions.com/what-is-the -leviathan-2076680.

9. "Hidden Symbols in the Loaves and Fish," First Fruits of Zion, accessed March 22, 2023, https://torahportions.ffoz.org/disciples/synoptic-gospels/hidden-symbols -in-the-loaves.html.

## Chapter 8: The Signs and Secrets of Sight

1. Nedarim 64b.

2. Alan Unterman, *Dictionary of Jewish Lore & Legend* (London: Thames & Hudson, 1991), eBook edition.

3. For more on this concept, read Pete Lange, "Scripture Interprets Scripture: What Does This Mean?" 1517: Christ for You, June 24, 2020, https://www.1517.org /articles/scripture-interprets-scripture-what-does-this-mean.

4. Rabbi Elie Munk, *The Call of the Torah: 2—Shemos* (New York: ArtScroll /Mesorah, 1994), 269.

5. Munk, *Call of the Torah: 2—Shemos*, 270.

6. Rabbi Shimon Schwab, *Rav Schwab on Yeshayahu* (Mesorah Publications, 2009), 388.

7. The Sefaria Midrash Rabbah, 1:15, 2022, https://www.sefaria.org/Eikhah_Rabbah .1.51?ven=The_Sefaria_Midrash_Rabbah,_2022&lang=bi.

8. The Sefaria Midrash Rabbah, 1:15.

9. Babylonian Talmud: Tractate Baba Bathra 126b.

10. There are several more phrases that equal 419: Psalm 95:3—"For *Adonai* is a great God and a great King above all gods." Psalm 29:3—"The God of glory thunders." Psalm 2:12—"Lest you perish."

11. Levi Avtzon, "The Clouds of Glory: What Were They?" Chabad.org, accessed March 23, 2023, https://www.chabad.org/parshah/article_cdo/aid/4305087 /jewish/The-Clouds-of-Glory-What-Were-They.htm.

12. Babylonian Talmud, Tractate *Sukkah* 51a and 51b.

13. "Radak on Genesis 11:9:1," Sefaria, accessed January 24, 2023, https://www .sefaria.org/Radak_on_Genesis.11.9.1?ven=Eliyahu_Munk,_HaChut _Hameshulash&lang=bi.

14. Pesikta Rabati ch. 37.

15. Ber. Rabba 1:6.

## Chapter 9: The Signs and Secrets of the Nets

1. W. E. Vine, Merrill F. Unger, and William White Jr., *Vine's Complete Expository Dictionary of Old and New Testament Words* (Nashville, TN: Thomas Nelson, 1996), Logos Bible Software Edition.

2. Different numbers are given, and one of those numbers is 153 portions over three and a half years. Jacob Neusner, *The Jerusalem Talmud* (Peabody, MA: Hendrickson, 2008), Logos Bible Software Edition.

3. Ronald L. Eisenberg, "The 13 Attributes of Mercy," My Jewish Learning, accessed January 10, 2023, https://www.myjewishlearning.com/article/the-13-attributes -of-mercy/.

4. "Luke 5," Pulpit Commentary, Bible Hub, accessed March 23, 2023, https:// biblehub.com/commentaries/pulpit/luke/5.htm, emphasis in the original.

5. "oneworld," accessed May 16, 2023, https://www.oneworld.com.

## Chapter 10: Is It Possible to Do Miracles Today?

1. John Wimber and Kevin Springer, *Power Evangelism* (Ventura, CA: Regal from Gospel Light, 2009), 38.

# ABOUT THE AUTHOR

**Rabbi Jason Sobel** is the founder of Fusion Global. This ministry seeks to bring people into the full inheritance of the faith by connecting treasures of the Old and the New. Rabbi Jason's voice is authentic, being raised in a Jewish home and qualified by years of diligent academic work. His voice is prophetic—touched by the life of the Spirit. He has a radical testimony of his supernatural encounter with Yeshua-Jesus. This moment awakened him to his calling and destiny.

Rabbi Jason received his rabbinic ordination from the UMJC (Union of Messianic Jewish Congregations) in 2005. He has a BA in Jewish studies (Moody) and an MA in intercultural studies (Southeastern Seminary). He is a sought-after speaker and has made multiple appearances on national television, including the Trinity Broadcasting Network, the Daystar Network, and the Dr. Oz Show. Rabbi Jason is the author of *Mysteries of the Messiah*; he is also the coauthor of the *New York Times* bestseller *The God of the Way* with Kathie Lee Gifford.

You can learn more at Rabbisobel.com or fusionglobal.org.

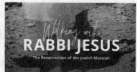

# EXPERIENCE THE LAND OF THE BIBLE
## IN HIGH DEFINITION

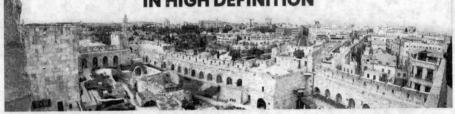

# Experience The Bible With Rabbi Jason Sobel

**Ready To Book A Life-Changing Experience?**

## ROCKROADRABBITOURS.COM

# JOURNEY DEEPER
## WITH RABBI JASON SOBEL

- **Add definition to your faith**
- **Restore the lost connection to your ancient roots**
- **Rediscover your forgotten inheritance**

Enrich your perspective of Yeshua-Jesus, His teaching, and His disciples by expanding your understanding of the Bible to include ancient Hebrew and contemporary wisdom, informed by the Spirit.

CONNECT DEEPER

@rabbijasonsobel

Learn how festivals, traditions, and Old Testament teachings are important to Jesus.
Together, let's grow to understand how important they should be to us as followers of Yeshua.

## JOURNEY DEEPER

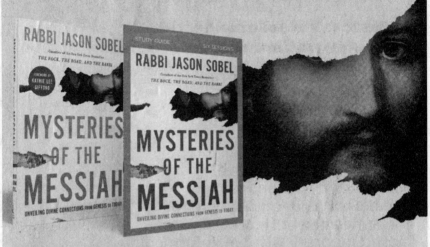